Dear Reader

The objective of Kendo World is to disseminate information that will help the international community of kendo aficionados in their study of the perennial path of traditional Japanese swordsmanship and related arts. Your purchase of this publication helps the Kendo World team travel around Japan to interview famous sensei, cover important kendo events, and pay translators for their tireless work deciphering kendo wisdom. We appreciate your continued support of Kendo World's aims to promote the beautiful art of kendo. If you are reading this publication on anything other than one of our authorised digital platforms (e.g. ZINIO, Kindle, iBooks), or in "Print on Demand" paper form via Amazon, then you are in possession of pirated material. As fellow kenshi, we appeal to your conscience in the hope that you refuse to participate in illegal file sharing of our copyrighted material. We agree that information belongs to everybody, but spare a thought for the time, effort, and resources that are required to bring it to you. Pirating is stealing. Without your backing, Kendo World will die. We don't want to die yet because there is still so much to do…

Happy reading and thank you.

Kendo World Team

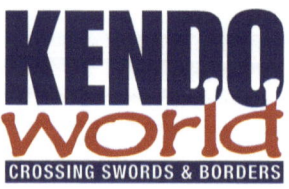

Carbon Shinai
カーボンシナイ

- CF-Type
- DB-Type
- K1-Type
- K2-Type

We have improved the official Carbon Shinai rubber stopper.

Orange   Red   Yellow

The NEW official rubber stopper.
¥300 (domestic Japanese price)

WARNING!! Never use anything other than our official rubber stopper on your Carbon Shinai !!
When using your Carbon Shinai.....

1. To prevent injury, please use our official rubber stopper. Do not use stoppers made for conventional bamboo shinai on your Carbon Shinai, as there is a risk of injury to your opponent if the tip breaks through and enters their men grill.
2. When choosing a sakigawa (leather tip), make sure that it is more than 5cm in length and completely covers our rubber stopper. If the sakigawa is shorter than 5cm, there is a risk of injury to your opponent if a slat slips out and enters their men grill.
3. Do not shave the plastic surface of your Carbon Shinai. If you shave the surface, the black carbon fiber will be exposed, causing damage that may result in injury to your opponent.
4. Always check the condition of the surface of your Carbon Shinai before and during use. As soon as you notice any cracks, or peeling of the surface, or if black carbon fiber is exposed on any part of the outside, inside or edges of the Shinai, or you notice any other damage, stop using the shinai immediately. There is a danger of injury to your opponent if your Carbon Shinai is split or broken.
5. When tying the nakayui (leather binding), either tie a knot in the tsuru-ito (cord), or tie one end of the nakayui to the tsuru-ito, or by another means ensuring that is does not move up and down during use. If there is any damage whatsoever to the sakigawa, tsukagawa (hilt), rubber stopper, tsuru-ito and so on, replace them immediately.
6. If the tip of the Carbon Shinai is damaged, or a slat is protuding out of the sakigawa, there is a danger that it could enter your opponent's men grill and injure them.

Kendogu Revolution

Mu-Jun Men
武楯面

WARNING!!

1. Under no circumstances should organic solvents (such as thinner, alcohol, benzene, toluene, acetone, gasoline, kerosene, etc.), acidic or alkali chemicals, domestic cleansers, car cleansers, or anti-mist sprays, be used to clean the shield. These substances will cause the shield to deteriorate, leading to clouding, cracking or breaking, thereby resulting in danger of injury to the face.
2. Should the shield develop deep scratches or cracks on either the outer or inner surface, discontinue use of the shield immediately, and replace it with an undamaged shield. If the shield is used in such a condition, there is a danger of it breaking, causing injury to the face.
3. It should be fully understood that, as with the traditional Japanese Kendo-Men (mask), there is still the danger of injury to the face through fragments of broken bamboo or Carbon Shinai pieces penetrating through areas not covered by the shield.

SG-Type

- SCIENCE TO SEEK SAFETY -

HASEGAWA
HASEGAWA CORPORATION

WEB : http://kendo.hasegawakagaku.co.jp
Email : contact@hasegawakagaku.co.jp

Carbon Shinai — Points to be checked

DANGER !!

ATTENTION !!

Before these happen.....

Although the Carbon Shinai is much more durable than a conventional bamboo one, it will inevitably become damaged since it is a sword that is used to repeatedly strike and thrust your opponent. Therefore, inspect the condition of the surface, sides or reverse of the Carbon Shinai's slats before, during and after use, and stop using it immediately should damage like in the following pictures be observed. (These pictures are just a few examples of many.)

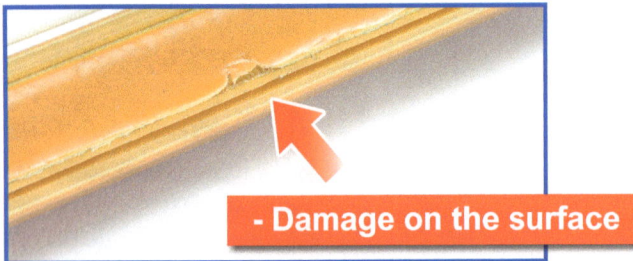
- Damage on the surface

- An unglued surface sheet

- Exposure of the Carbon fiber

- Longitudinal crack on the surface

- Damage and ungluing of the surface

- Crack on the reverse

There is the case where the reverse gets cracked even without any damage on the surface. Inspect the inside of the Shinai by pushing the pieces with the fingers and unbinding the Naka-yui.

HASEGAWA-KOTE

- Detachable and washable "Tenouchi" is easy to wash and dry.
- "Tenouchi" is replaceable when torn. No need to repair.

Tenouchi (Inner)

Kote (Main part)

- SCIENCE TO SEEK SAFETY -

HASEGAWA CORPORATION
http://kendo.hasegawakagaku.co.jp/

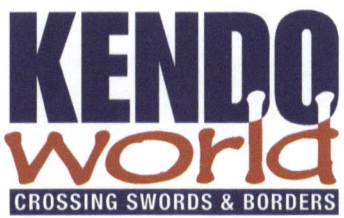

PUBLICATIONS

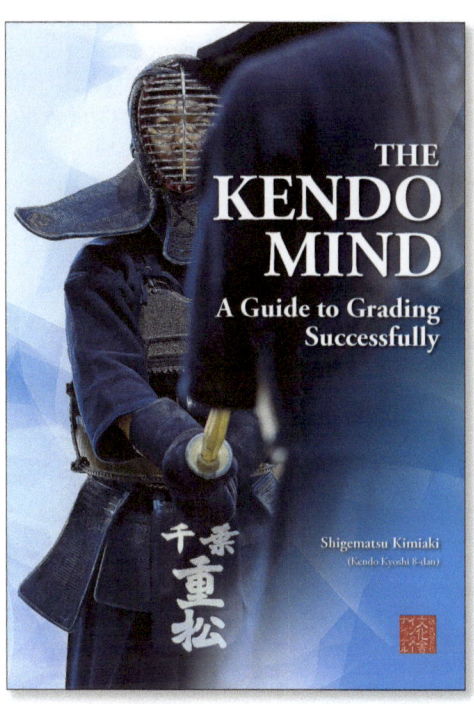

Naginata
Naginata, History and Practice

Of the handful of books on Naginata that do exist, most are prewar Japanese textbooks which are for the most part irrelevant to the popular form of Naginata developed in the post-war period. Postwar Naginata books are scant, and usually only cover the same basic techniques. Very little information is offered in regards to the cultural, historical, and mental aspects of Naginata. It requires a concerted effort to find such information in Japanese books, and to date, apart from a few journal articles, there has been virtually no work done in these areas in English or any other language. Until now, Naginata practitioners around the world have been left almost completely in the dark with regard to how the modern art that we practise today actually evolved and took its current form, in a process that spanned over one thousand years. This book fills the gap.

The Kendo Mind:
A Guide to Grading Successfully

Those who study kendo regard examinations and matches as vehicles for cultivating self-discipline and skill. Preparing to take a grading is especially motivating compared to regular training. It is, however, also a tremendous disappointment when you fail. There are those who manage to pass each examination without ever failing, and others who reach an impasse. So, what is the difference between these two groups? If you can figure it out, even just a little, you are one step closer to finding success. There are many things needed to pass an examination, not least of which is impressing the judges with resonating strikes. There is no way to achieve your goal without knowing how to accomplish this. The content of this book is based on lessons I learned from my sensei, my personal experiences in the dojo, and what I read in books and instruction manuals along the way. I hope that you will find the information in this small volume useful reference material as you navigate the path of kendo.

More info → www.kendo-world.com

KENDO WORLD Volume 8.3 December 2016 Contents

Editorial Letting Go…	2
The 64th All Japan Kendo Championships	4
Kendo as Music; Music as Kendo	18
Uncle Kotay's Kendo Korner Part 3: The Three Initiatives	21
The Philosophy of Miyamoto Musashi's Gorin-no-sho	22
Kendo for Adults	29
From Katate Guntō-jutsu to Tanken-jutsu: The birth of Tankendo	32
Dojo File Phnom Penh Kendo Club	37
The Shugyō Mind: Part 3	38
Reidan-jichi Part 22 **Various Shikake-waza**	40
sWords of Wisdom "Jippatsu kyū-chū"	42
Yamamoto Mariko Seminar	44
A Guide to Japanese Armour	48
The 2016 Shūdōkai Grading Gasshuku	52
Guidelines to Kendo Promotional Examinations Part 1	58
Inishie wo Kangaeru	64
Tendō-ryū	66
Hagakure and the Perennial Path to Perfection	71
Takano Sasaburō's *Kendō*	72
Bujutsu Jargon Part 10	76
ShinaiSagas Seven Meditations	78
Musō Jikiden Eishin-ryū Riai The Meaning of the Kata: Part 5	82
The Year that was 2016	89

Kendo World Staff
- Bunkasha International President & Editor-in-Chief— Alex Bennett PhD
- Bunkasha International Vice President & Assistant Editor—Michael Ishimatsu-Prime MA
- Bunkasha International Vice President & Graphic Design—Shishikura 'Kan' Masashi
- Bunkasha International Vice President—Hamish Robison
- Bunkasha International Vice President—Michael Komoto MA
- Bunkasha International General Manager—Baptiste Tavernier MA
- Senior Consultants—Yonemoto Masayuki, Shima Masahiko

KW Staff Writers / Translators / Photographers / Graphic Designer / Sub-editors

- Axel Pilgrim PhD
- Blake Bennett PhD
- Bruce Flanagan MA
- Bryan Peterson
- Charlie Kondek
- Gabriel Weitzner
- Honda Sōtarō PhD
- Imafuji Masahiro MBA
- Jeff Broderick
- Kate Sylvester PhD
- Okuura Ayako
- Sergio Boffa PhD
- Stephen Nagy PhD
- Steven Harwood MA
- Takubo Seiya
- Taylor Winter
- Tony Cundy
- Trevor Jones
- Tyler Rothmar
- Yamaguchi Remi
- Vivian Yung
- Yulin Zhuang

KW would like to thank the following people and organisations for their valuable cooperation:
- All Japan Kendo Federation
- Hasegawa Teiichi - President, Hasegawa Corporation
- *Kendo Jidai* Magazine
- *Kendo Nihon* Magazine
- Nippon Budokan Foundation
- Nine Circles
- Shogun Kendogu
- TOZANDO

Guest Writers
- Diana C. Kitthajaroenchai (Georgia Kendo Association)
- Hatano Toshio (Kendo Kyōshi 8-dan)
- Jeff Marsten (Kendo Kyōshi 7-dan, PNKF)
- J. Michael Sills (Phnom Penh Kendo Club)
- Jo Anseeuw (Association for the Research and Preservation of Japanese Helmets and Armour)
- Kim Taylor (Iaido 7-dan, sdksupplies.com)
- Kimura Yasuko (17th Sōke of Tendō-ryū)
- Mutō Kazuhiro (Kendo Kyōshi 8-dan)
- Orikasa Teruo (Association for the Research and Preservation of Japanese Helmets and Armour)
- Ōya Minoru (Prof. International Budo University; Kendo Kyōshi 7-dan)
- Shigematsu Kimiaki (Kendo Kyōshi 8-dan)
- Uozumi Takashi (Open University, Japan)

COPYRIGHT 2017 Bunkasha International Corporation. No part of this publication may be reproduced in any form whatsoever without written permission from the publisher, except by writers who are permitted to quote brief passages for the purpose of review or reference. Kindly contact Bunkasha International Corporation at info@kendo-world.com.

Editorial Conventions Used in KW Inevitably in a magazine of this nature, many non-English words appear in the text. All Japanese words are italicised and include macrons (ū, ō) etc., apart from common place names and nouns, and words in some captions and headings. As a general exception, KW treats all the martial arts (budo), such as kendo, iaido, jodo, ranks, and so on as Anglicised words without using macrons. Japanese names are written in accordance to the traditional Japanese manner of family name followed by given name. Traditional *ryūha* are written with capitals and therefore are not italicised. 'Kata' with a capital 'K' refers to the set of Nippon Kendo Kata, and *kata* refers to set forms in general. The masculine personal pronoun is used throughout the text in some articles in the interest of readability, and is in no way meant to slight the significant contributions made by female kendoka.

Editorial
Letting Go… By Alex Bennett

I was lining up for *keiko* with Shigematsu Kimiaki-sensei (K8-dan) in Chiba recently, where the KW Team had gathered for the KW Gasshuku to get this magazine ready for print. The person before me who was already engaged in *keiko* was a KW Team member. He is a serious young man who aspires to do orthodox kendo. As I watched the *keiko*, trying to prepare my mind for my own impending doom, I found myself muttering about the young fella's kendo. I could see that he was doing his best to keep it together, but he was totally missing the point in more ways than one. I kept saying to him under my breath, "Go now! Now…! Goddammit! Now… Now!" I was imagining myself in his shoes, and watching how Shigematsu-sensei was trying to encourage him to let go, but to no avail. The openings were being presented for the taking, if only he would just get over his preoccupation with trying to score a point. All he attempted to do was pick off a lucky *debana-kote* or two and try to look conventional…

I could see that Shigematsu-sensei was getting frustrated. The young fella was not jamming on stage, he was just trying to play his own solo tune. It got me thinking about the correct way to do *keiko*, especially against a sensei. The lad in question has probably never been told this before, so this Editorial is for him.

It takes two to tango, and *keiko* is the time where you dance until the cows come home. We are often told that when facing a sensei, no matter how great, you should always try to score the first point. It doesn't have to be pretty, just be bloody tenacious and as competitive as you can be. The first point is a competition, a fight to the death.

Then, come what may, you use the sensei to guide you to a different place. That's what sensei do. When you know that the technical gap is immense, and your best efforts at taking *ippon* are not working, just let go and enjoy the ride.

It doesn't have to be *kakari-geiko* straight off the bat, but you should always look to take the initiative and attack, attack, attack. You might get *kaeshi-do*'d, *nuki-do*'d, *ai-men*'d, *debana-kote*'d, *mukai-tsuki*'d, and smashed into the wall. Who cares? Learning to let go is possibly one of the hardest parts of kendo, but when you finally do, it is incredibly liberating. Sure, it's hard work, but the level of discomfort is commensurate to the amount of post-*keiko* euphoria. And, it really is the ONLY way to improve. Learn all the techniques in the world to absolute perfection; if you can't let go when the time comes, they will be of no use whatsoever.

Letting go is "*sutemi*", which literally means "discarding the body". It is a common word in the parlance of kendo and other martial arts. It teaches the magnitude of sacrificing yourself fully into the attack—expunging any tentativeness and striking with total conviction the instant opportunity knocks. This, of course, is easier said than done. Until people "let go" and take the plunge, they are debilitated by their anxiety of the consequences, or obsessed with somehow making the *shinai* touch the target. It might, but it will be devoid of "oomph".

What is needed to make *keiko* against sensei worth everybody's while is the conviction, courage, and confidence engendered by "*sutemi*", and to be unfazed by whatever you *imagine* might befall you. Sensei has got your best interests at heart. After contesting the first point, just let go and jam. When the moment is right, there is no time to waste thinking about all the "what ifs".

I am reminded of another keyword associated with this mindset, "*shini-gurui*". This is a term which I translate as "death frenzy", and appears often in the old bushido classic, *Hagakure*. This phrase may seem somewhat alarming, but I think of it as the mental attitude that underpins *sutemi*. Figuratively speaking, "death frenzy" does not mean you are hellbent on dying, or killing for that matter. It means drawing on a latent internal power so great that it elevates you to a different plane of being, and enables you to accomplish whatever it is that you need to do. It means being able to face danger directly, and acting with the force of *sutemi* without hesitating. To achieve this state, you must be resigned to the possibility that you may very well be hit in the process. If you are going to get hit anyway, it is better to go in a blaze of glory.

Ideally, this kind of *keiko* will morph into *kakari-geiko* as a natural progression, and the jam will reach its crescendo. Watch the smile on your sensei's face when you strike that last *men* with sheer determination. Watch how much progress you make in your kendo from then on. "Go now!"

Katsumi Yōsuke—the 64th All Japan Champion

The 64th All Japan Kendo Championships
Thursday November 3, 2016

Report by Michael Ishimatsu-Prime
Additional material by K8-dan Shigematsu Kimiaki

The 64th AJKC proved to be another tournament in which the younger generation of kenshi continue to outdo their seniors in the most prestigious kendo tournament in Japan. Before we look at who was there, let us take a look at who was not. The most notable absence was Uchimura Ryōichi, champion in 2006, 2009, and 2013. Between 2005 and 2013, only once did Uchimura not qualify (2008), and only once did he not finish in the medal places (2007; best-8), with three championships, three runner-ups, and one third-place in that period: a fantastic record. He has not fared as well in the last two championships, losing in the third-round in 2014 to Takeshita Yōhei (Oita), and then in 2015 in the second round to Kitaura Yūsuke (Nagasaki). Tokyo takes four of the 64 slots available for the AJKC, but Uchimura finished in fifth place in the Tokyo qualifying tournament. He is now 36 years of age, so he is undoubtedly towards

the end of his All-Japan competitive career, but this is the same age that Miyazaki Masahiro won the last of his six titles. Miyazaki then qualified for the two following AJKCs, finishing third and losing in the second round, so we may well see Uchimura in the AJKC again.

Another notable absence was Takenouchi Yūya. He set the kendo world alight when, as a third-year student at the University of Tsukuba, he won the AJKC on his debut becoming the youngest ever champion at 21 years and five months. He qualified as the Fukuoka representative again the following year, but was knocked out in the third round. He has been a member of Keishichō (Tokyo Police) since April 2016 after graduating, and so now must go through the Tokyo qualifying tournament. He lost in the fifth round of the qualifying tournament to police officer Orita Shōhei.

Table 1 shows the line-up of the competitors that qualified for the 64th AJKC.

As usual, police officers made up the majority of competitors, up three from the previous year. This is the second year in a row that seven of the 64 competitors that qualified were teachers. Company workers were down from four to two.

In recent years, it has been more common to see students in the AJKC, starting in 2008 with Hatakenaka Kōsuke, a fourth-year Kokushikan University student who represented Wakayama prefecture. Before Hatakenaka, the last student to qualify did so 30 years before him in 1978 at the 26th AJKC. That was 4-dan Kōda Kunihide (21) from the University of Tsukuba who represented Ibaraki; he finished in third place. Kōda-sensei is now K8-dan and is actually a professor at Tsukuba where he has guided both the men's and women's teams to eight victories each in the All Japan Student Team Championships.

Hatakenaka is now a police officer in Tokyo, and won the Tokyo qualifying tournament this year. Since then, there have been Andō Shō (Kokushikan University but now Hokkaido police), Osonoi Naoki (third in this year's Tokyo qualifier but made his debut as a fourth-year Tsukuba student), Umegatani Kakeru (a second-year Chuo University student representing Fukuoka who finished third in 2015) and Sanada Hiroyuki (a Kanoya University second-year student who qualified via Tottori prefecture), and of course Takenouchi.

The trend of students qualifying continued in the 64th AJKC with two in the final 64. The aforementioned Sanada qualified again, this time as a 4-dan. So too did Miyamoto Keita (4-dan), a third-year Kokushikan University student representing Ibaraki prefecture. Sanada made it to the second-round last year, and is a competitor with real pedigree. He had already won and finished as runner-up in the Student Team Championships, and won the Inter-High Team event. Miyamoto has competed in both the team and individual student championships.

Nishimura Hidehisa, the 2015 champion, qualified again. Last year he used his *shinai*-hooking technique from *tsubazeriai* to great effect. Nishimura's preferred technique is *kote*, and it is likely his opponents anticipate attacks will come from there. In fact, in 2015, all the *ippon* he scored up until the final were *kote*, but in the championship match against Katsumi Yōsuke (Kanagawa) he scored two spectacular *men*

(Table 1) Number of Competitors by Profession				
Police Officers	Teachers	Prison Officers	Company Workers	Students
50	7	3	2	2

(Table 2) Number of Student Competitors								
56th (2008)	57th (2009)	58th (2010)	59th (2011)	60th (2012)	61st (2013)	62nd (2014)	63rd (2015)	64th (2016)
1	–	1	2	1	–	4	3	2

through varying his approach. In his pre-tournament notes written for the AJKF homepage, H8-dan Masago Takeshi-sensei said of Nishimura:

"He is an outstanding competitor. His *men* that doesn't look like it will be *men*; his *kote* attack that comes from below; his ability to freely attack from above or below, *omote* or *ura*; coupled with his ability to launch amazing *hiki-waza* techniques from *tsubazeriai*, give him a good chance of winning. He has the skills necessary to be champion again this year."

Other kenshi that Masago-sensei thought would have a chance to go all the way were the 2015 defeated finalist, 5-dan Katsumi Yōsuke (Kanagawa), who qualified this year to make his third appearance in the finals; Kunitomo Rentarō, a debutant and runner-up in 2014 who is well known for his strong *kamae* and not stepping back when under pressure; and Shōdai Masahiro (R6-dan, Tokyo) who was in great form at the 2015 WKC.

The KW Commentary Team: (l-r) Shigematsu Kimiaki-sensei, Alex Bennett, Michael Ishimatsu-Prime

Other notable entrants were R6-dan Hatakenaka Kōsuke (Tokyo), third place in 2014; 5-dan Andō Shō (Hokkaido) who lost to Nishimura at the quarter-final stage in 2015; and R7-dan Higashinaga Yukihiro (Saitama), runner-up in 2011 who is appearing in the AJKC for the tenth time.

The first round of the 64th All Japan Kendo Championships certainly had its fair share of shocks. Osaka is traditionally one of the strongest prefectures, demonstrated by the fact that they have taken the Police Team Championships three times over the past five years. Osaka's three entrants were Tsuchitani Yūki (4-dan), Ejima Kazuharu (5-dan), and Masuda Ryō (5-dan), the former two making their debut, and the latter his second. In terms of the AJKC, this was a very fresh line-up from Osaka. However, Tsuchitani won the Police Individual Championships in 2015; Masuda the WKC Team Championships twice and the Police Team Championships three times; and Ejima has won the Police Team Championships twice. Tsuchitani was pitted against Kamiuto Tesshū (5-dan, Kagoshima) in the first round, and was defeated by *men* in *enchō*. Masuda fought against Kinoshita Tomonari (R6-dan, Kagawa), also losing by a *men* strike in *enchō*. It was therefore left to Ejima to fly the flag for Osaka.

There were more competitors you would expect to make it to the later stages who had their tournament cut short in the first round. Andō Shō was defeated by Tokyo's Osonoi Naoki (5-dan, Tokyo); 6-dan Harada Kenji (Fukushima) in his eleventh appearance fell to Shōdai Masahiro; and Higashinaga Yukihiro lost

Higashinaga goes for *men* against Kenjō (1R)

Student Miyamoto tries *katsugi-waza* against Kusanagi (1R)

to a debutant in the first round—24-year-old Kenjō Naoki (4-dan, Fukuoka).

The second round also saw a big surprise: Shōdai, one of the tournament favourites, lost to Nishimura Takeshi (R6-dan, Hyogo) by a solitary *men* strike, and therefore missed out on the chance to be the first husband and wife All Japan Champions following his wife Sayuri's victory in the women's competition in 2016.

More competitors with a good chance of progressing to the later stages who also fell in the second round were as follows: R6-dan Nishiyama Hirokazu in his fourth outing was defeated by student Miyamoto

Hioki attacks Ebihara (1R)

Andō attempts *men* against Osonoi (1R)

Kashihara on the defensive against Suzuki (1R)

Ōishi attempts *hiki-men* against Nishino (1R)

Araki tries *dō* against Satō (1R)

Shōdai (l) faces Harada (1R)

Keita; Sanada, the other student, bested Osonoi; and 6-dan Kotani Akinori, runner-up in 2013, fell to Hatakenaka.

Moving into the third round, only one of Osaka's three entrants was left (Ejima), and one of Tokyo's four (Hatakenaka); but both of Kanagawa's (5-dan Takami Masaru and 5-dan Katsumi Yōsuke) remained. After a poor AJKC in 2011, all of the Tokyo entrants were dropped from the Tokuren (Keishicho's elite kendo squad) with the exception of Uchimura who was promoted to captain. By the end of the third round in 2016, however, Tokyo had lost all of its competitors with the defeat of Hatakenaka to Katsumi. One wonders how the Tokuren will react this time following these disappointing results. Also, Kanagawa's Takami was defeated by the debutant from Saitama, 5-dan Adachi Ryūji. Osaka's Ejima finished Sanada's second AJKC with a *dō* strike. Sanada, a third-year Kanoya student, went one round better than he did in 2015, so it will be interesting how far he can go if he qualifies again next year as a fourth-year student.

Koshikawa (l) launches an attack on Kitaura (2R)

Sanada (r) the student defends himself against Ejima (3R)

Katsumi strikes Hatakenaka's *men* as he attempts *gyaku-dō* (3R)

Kotani (l) and Hatakenaka trying to find an opening (2R)

Kunitomo (l) pressures Nishimura (3R)

Adachi (l) attacks Jishiro's *men* (QF1)

Adachi (r) attacks Jishiro's *men* (QF1)

The quarter-finals had a fresh feel to them. In QF1, Adachi was making his debut and Jishiro Mitsuhiro (5-dan, Hokkaido) his second appearance. In QF2, Nishimura was in his third AJKC, and Kunitomo his second. In QF3, both Miyamoto and Ejima were debutants; and in QF4, 5-dan Ōishi Hiroshi (Tokushima) was in his first AJKC against Katsumi in his third. Katsumi had made it to the best-8 in his first appearance, and runner-up in his second.

Adachi made it to the quarter-final by winning each of his first three matches with *ippon* victories with *men*. In the first round against 4-dan Naitō Hiroshi (Fukui), Adachi scored a *hiki-men* after his opponent went for *dō* but stopped after making contact. In the second round when he faced Kagoshima's Kamiuto Tesshū (5-dan), Adachi again seized on his opponent's hesitation and scored another *men* about halfway through the encounter. It took about seven minutes of *enchō* for Adachi to overcome Kanagawa's Takami, and he did it with *men*. Takami pressured, moved back, but as he moved forward again, Adachi was ready.

Jishiro's road to the quarter-final was an *enchō* victory against Sakaguchi Hiroshi (5-dan, Kyoto) with a *men* strike; another *men* just before the end of regulation time against Hioki Yasunori (R6-dan, Aichi); and a lightning-fast *kote* in *enchō* against Kitaura Yūsuke (5-dan, Nagasaki) who, as noted above, defeated Uchimura in the second round in 2015.

Adachi is known for his strong *men*, *kote* and *dō*, and Jishiro for his formidable *men* strike, as was evident in his second-round match against Hioki. Because Adachi was the smaller of the two, he needed to pressure Jishiro from above, or he would be easily struck. For the first couple of minutes, Adachi was pressuring *kote* from below, but he perhaps would have been wiser to attack from above (according to KW commentator, Shigematsu-sensei). He kept pressuring *kote*, but that was risky against someone with such a powerful *men* as Jishiro. Adachi was the more active and was attempting more techniques. Because Jishiro is so good at *men*, he was attempting *kote* to make Adachi think that there was danger there, too. The tactic paid off. When Jishiro dropped the tip of his *shinai* and changed from *omote* to *ura*, Adachi thought *kote* was coming but Jishiro chose this moment to go for *men*. *Ippon*. Soon after, Jishiro tried the same tactic but struck *kote* instead, scoring his second *ippon*. Jishiro did not attack much, but had the perfect balance of *seme*: pressure *kote*, but strike *men*; and vice versa.

QF2 featured defending champion Nishimura Hidehisa and the defeated 2014 finalist, Kunitomo Rentarō. Nishimura's trademark technique is *kote*, which he used so effectively in the 2015 AJKC (except for in the final when he surprised Katsumi and won with two *men* strikes). It should therefore come as no surprise that his first three matches against Iwasaki Ryūichirō (5-dan, Iwate), Oike Tomoyuki (6-dan, Okayama), and Kinoshita Tomonari (R6-dan, Kagawa) were all won with *kote* strikes. Kunitomo, like Nishimura, used his preferred technique (*men*) to get *ippon* throughout the first three rounds, beating 6-dan Yamamoto Takahiro (Hiroshima), 4-dan Satō Hirotaka (Chiba), and R6-dan Nishimura Takeshi (Hyogo), with *men* in *enchō*. This seems to be quite indicative of Kunitomo's kendo: he does not rush in, but bides his time and waits for the perfect opportunity.

As the defending champion, Nishimura was the favourite in this quarter-final. Nishimura and Kunitomo met in the semi-final of the AJKC in 2014 in which the latter won in *enchō* with *men*. In this encounter, it was Kunitomo who made the first good attempt at *ippon*. As Nishimura moved in and changed from *omote* to *ura* he paused slightly, to which Kunitomo seized the moment to go for *men*, albeit unsuccessfully. They ended up in *tsubazeriai*, and obviously cognizant of the damage Nishimura did from that position last year, Kunitomo separated very cautiously.

Before the match began, Kendo World commentator K8-dan Shigematsu Kimiaki-sensei commented that Nishimura would probably attack more, and that Kunitomo will probably hold back and wait for the perfect opportunity. Three minutes in and that is exactly what was happening. Nishimura's attacks were not finding a way through Kunitomo's strong *kamae*. Nishimura unleashed a trademark *kote*—moving up to strike *men*, but quickly bringing it down for *kote*— but it did not score. To get around Kunitomo's *kamae*, Nishimura was varying his angle of *kote* attack. Kunitomo was ready, and scored a beautiful *men*.

The pace picked up a bit after that *ippon*, but it was Kunitomo who had the best chance: a *hiki-men*. Nishimura began to go for more *kote* attacks, but could not score. Kunitomo had to be careful as Nishimura was coming in from all angles. It looked like Nishimura's multi-angle approach was running

Defending champion Nishimura (l) tries to strike Kunitomo's *kote* (QF2)

Ejima (l) and Miyamoto (third-year Kokushikan student) in *tsubazeriai* (QF3)

Miyamoto (l) attacks Ejima's *kote* (QF3)

out of ideas; his *kote* was becoming *katsugi-waza*, but again Kunitomo was ready. Nishimura tried a small *harai* from *omote* to knock Kunitomo's *shinai* off the centre, most likely to try and draw him into attacking *men* so he could go for *kote*. Kunitomo held firm, moved his *shinai* under Nishimura's to take back the centre, and as Nishimura felt compelled to attempt *men*, Kunitomo scored a great *de-gote* to progress to the semi-final.

In QF3, the Kokushikan student Miyamoto faced the policeman Ejima. Out of the 64 competitors in this AJKC, there were ten Kokushikan graduates, plus Miyamoto who is still a student there. The next best represented university was Tsukuba with eight, and then Kanoya (National Institute of Fitness and Sports in Kanoya) with six; so, alumni of those three college kendo powerhouses account for almost 40 per cent of the competitors this year.

Like Takenouchi two years earlier, Miyamoto was something of a revelation. It looked as if his opponents could not deal with his speed, and his willingness to keep going for the second *ippon* without sitting back and defending his advantage. Miyamoto was actually the only quarter-finalist who did not need *enchō* to decide any of his earlier matches, winning by either *ippon-gachi* or two *ippon*.

Miyamoto after his QF victory against Ejima (QF3)

Ejima was Osaka's only representative left. The last time Osaka had a winner was at the 60th champs with Kiwada Daisuke. It was up to Ejima to restore the pride of Osaka. The match started at a furious pace with an *ai-men* as soon as they stood up. Miyamoto got in five strikes within the first ten seconds, and Ejima three. The match settled down slightly, and Ejima struck *men*. One flag went up, but the other two *shinpan* waved it off.

From the outset, Miyamoto had strong feeling to his kendo. Shigematsu-sensei commented that Ejima has a typical "Osaka-style" kendo: his feet are always on

Oishi (r) pressures Katsumi (QF4)

the move. As soon as they stop moving, however, that creates an opening. About three minutes into the match, Miyamoto made another two good attempts at *men*, but no flags. After a short spell in *tsubazeriai*, Ejima nods his head to signal that they should separate. As soon as they do, Miyamoto moves in. Ejima's feet are static and the *de-gote* he tries does not connect as Miyamoto comes forward with *men* to score.

The quarter-finals are ten minutes long, and there were still about six minutes remaining. Defending that lead would be very hard, but that is not Miyamoto's style anyway. Right after the restart he attempts *kote* and then *men*. While separating from *tsubazeriai*, Miyamoto goes for a cheeky *men* strike, but it does not really connect. Ejima keeps retreating to open up the *maai*, but Miyamoto just pulls his right foot back slightly while keeping his left still, primed, and ready to go. Just as Ejima begins to advance, Miyamoto launches himself forward and strikes *men*. Maybe Ejima's ploy was to lure Miyamoto into striking *men* so that he could capture a *kote*. He had a much better attempt this time and got one flag, but Miyamoto's

men was solid, resolute, and the other two *shinpan* raised their flags for him. According to Ejima's profile, his preferred technique is *kote*, but in the AJKC he failed to score with a single one, winning his first three matches with *dō*, *men*, and *dō*.

QF4 featured 30-year-old debutant Ōishi Hiroshi (5-dan, Tokushima), and Katsumi Yōsuke. Ōishi is a 30-year-old middle and senior high school teacher who was a graduate of Osaka University of Health and Sports Sciences. Even though this is his first AJKC, he nonetheless has an impressive competitive history. He was runner-up in both the team and individual competitions of the All Japan Student Championships, has placed third in the Todōfūken, won the Kokutai (National Sports Meet), placed third in the All Japan Teacher's Championships team event, and is the current individual champion in the Teachers of Compulsory Education division.

In the first two rounds Ōishi beat Nishino Tetsuya (4-dan, Niigata) and Kashihara Keisuke (4-dan, Shiga), with *men* in *enchō*, and then a *kote* and *men* respectively. In the third round, he met the

Kunitomo attacks Jishiro's *men* (SF1)

Kunitomo attacks Jishiro's *kote* (SF1)

oldest competitor in the AJKC, 39-year-old R7-dan Kawaki Kazuya of Yamagata who was in his seventh championships. He won that encounter with a solid *hiki-men*.

Ōishi is a good deal taller than Katsumi, as he was with the rest of his opponents. Before the match started, Shigematsu-sensei thought that because of his size, Ōishi will most likely concentrate on *men*, but as Katsumi has speed, he will try and use that to capitalise on openings when they arise. For the opening exchanges, Ōishi attacked from out far, but as the match wore on, Katsumi managed to close the distance. Katsumi seemed to be pressuring Ōishi more to make him attack. He made Ōishi commit to a *dō* strike, and scored *hiki-men*. Almost straight after the restart, Katsumi throws himself into a *men* strike and scores to set up a semi-final clash with Miyamoto.

The first semi-final was between Jishiro and Kunitomo, both of whom are Kokushikan University graduates. They both have physically dominating styles, and before the match began, Shigematsu-sensei thought that it would be fought from *tōma*. He thought that Jishiro would possibly try an all-out attack on *kote* to make Kunitomo think that technique was a danger, but then go for one of his trademark *men*. He also commented that even though Kunitomo is young, he has a kendo level beyond his years: it is very orthodox.

The first few minutes of the match were even, with no real clear chances for either competitor. While there was the occasional attempt at *kote*, they were both focusing on *men* but they were not closing much because they were very wary of each other. Kunitomo started to pressure Jishiro by striking *kote*, which upset Jishiro's rhythm, but nothing came to a point in match time.

Regulation time ended and the match headed into *enchō*. In the previous ten minutes, neither Katsumi nor Kunitomo came close to dropping their concentration. As *enchō* started, Jishiro seemed to be the more confident of the two, as holes were starting to appear in Kunitomo's defence. Kunitomo attempted *tsuki*, but to no avail. The tide then started to turn in Jishiro's favour, but Kunitomo was still dangerous as he pressured Jishiro, who then attempted *men*. Kunitomo scored a beautiful *men-kaeshi-dō*. Kunitomo's left foot never moved back, even when pressured, which made him very strong. In his second AJKC, Kunitomo made it to his second final.

Jishiro (l) and Kunitomo in *tsubazeriai* (SF1)

Kunitomo scores *dō ippon* against Jishiro (SF1)

In the second semi-final, Miyamoto faced Katsumi. Miyamoto had a height advantage so it was important that Katsumi fully committed to each strike. Katsumi has a massive repertoire of techniques to fall back on, but Miyamoto, being a student, had nothing to lose. To get to the semi-final in his first AJKC, and as a student, he had already stamped his mark. Shigematsu-sensei thought that Katsumi's plan would be to make Miyamoto do something out of his comfort zone.

Again, as soon as he stood up from *sonkyo*, Miyamoto went for Katsumi's *men*. Soon after, Miyamoto tried for *tsuki*, then *kote*, and then *men*. It was all Miyamoto for about the first minute. Katsumi was being very cautious when separating from *tsubazeriai*, maybe after seeing that Miyamoto would attempt to strike as they separated. Miyamoto was holding fast under Katsumi's *seme*, and had another good attempt at *men*, which Katsumi could not counter, but it was not scored. Katsumi started to attack more after about the three-minute mark, but Miyamoto was still a threat.

At around the 3m30s mark while they were at *issoku-ittō-no-maai*, Katsumi moved his right foot in, Miyamoto followed but held his position even though his right foot kept moving forward very slowly. Katsumi, again moved his right foot in slightly, but Miyamoto saw the opportunity and launched himself forward to score *men*, just a fraction quicker than Katsumi. Katsumi was maybe expecting Miyamoto to come quicker, but he misread him and conceded an *ippon*.

With still more than six minutes on the clock remaining, Katsumi did not really need to rush. Miyamoto could not defend that lead and had to keep attacking. After that *ippon*, however, it was Katsumi that was doing all the running while Miyamoto seemed content to sit back a little. Katsumi had a very good shout for *men* that excited the crowd, but not the *shinpan*. After a *kote* attempt by Miyamoto, Katsumi again went for *men*. And again.

Katsumi closed the *maai* and lured Miyamoto into going for a weak *kote*. Katsumi was ready and countered with a great *kote-kaeshi-men* to even the match. Both moved in at the restart. Miyamoto dropped his *kensen* and then landed what looked like a decisive *tsuki*. As Katsumi was pushed back he struck *hiki-men*. Miyamoto, and probably most of the

Miyamoto (r) attacks Katsumi's *men* (SF2)

Katsumi (r) launches a *men* attack against Miyamoto (SF2)

crowd at the Nippon Budokan, thought that *tsuki* was the winner, but three white flags for Katsumi went up.

A *Kendo World* team member belongs to the same dojo as one of the *shinpan* from that match. He, and other dojo members, asked why Katsumi's *hiki-men* was given and not Miyamoto's *tsuki*. Apparently, it was because Miyamoto should have withdrawn after landing the *tsuki*. Instead, he kept moving forward which enabled Katsumi to strike *hiki-men*.

The only *tsuki* that was judged *ippon* in this AJKC was scored by Tokyo's R6-dan Koshikawa Kazutaka against R6-dan Hashimoto Hiromi (Yamaguchi) in their first-round match. In that, Koshikawa withdrew after making contact and did not give Hashimoto the opportunity to attack. In essence, by moving forward too much after the *tsuki*, Miyamoto was not displaying proper *zanshin*…

Regardless, this was a fantastic semi-final and Miyamoto did exceptionally well. It appeared that his opponents could not manage his intensity and speed. He will make a great addition to any of the Tokuren teams, and it would be no surprise if they are already trying to sign him up.

Now the final. Both Katsumi and Kunitomo were runners-up in their previous AJKC, in 2015 and 2014 respectively. Both are members of the Japanese national team training squad, so they know each other well. According to Shigematsu-sensei, this final was going to be a clash of styles with Kunitomo most likely keeping straight and holding back for the perfect opportunity, and Katsumi probably trying to attack from all angles.

The first exchange proved to be consistent with Shigematsu-sensei's prediction: Kunitomo held firm only adjusting his position to match the angles that Katsumi was coming from. From the outset, Katsumi was letting go with more techniques than Kunitomo. Within the first three minutes, Kunitomo only made about three strikes, considerably less than Katsumi. Kunitomo's pressure always led to an attack with no hint of defence. His left foot never once moved back.

In the seventh minute, Katsumi finally found a way through Kunitomo's *kamae*. Katsumi kept moving in and out, changing from *omote* to *ura*. He looked like he was about to launch a *men* attack from *omote*, but instead went over the top of Kunitomo's *shinai* and scored *kote*. Kunitomo's right foot was caught flat on the floor,

Kunitomo (r) ready to counter a Katsumi attack

Katsumi (r) strikes Kunitomo's *kote*

and too far forward to be able to counter effectively. He managed to strike *kote* and *hiki-men*, but Katsumi's *kote* was solid and he closed so quickly that they were never going to score. It was a great *kote* from Katsumi.

After that *ippon*, three minutes remained. It was Kunitomo who attacked first after the restart, and he was being more aggressive than earlier in the match. Katsumi needed to keep the pressure on. He made a good attempt at *tsuki*, but the *shinpan* did not acknowledge it. Katsumi went for the same type of *kote* strike that he scored earlier. Kunitomo was ready, and countered with an unsuccessful *men* strike.

As the buzzer sounded, Katsumi became the 64th All-Japan Champion. In only his second AJKC appearance, Kunitomo made it to the final, for the second time, and as he is only 26, he will undoubtedly be one to watch in the future. Also worthy of special mention are the two students, Miyamoto Keita and Sanada Hiroyuki, and the teacher Ōishi Hiroshi who all have a very beautiful style of kendo. Both Miyamoto and Sanada will most likely be back in future AJKCs. If Sanada makes it again next year, he will have qualified as a second-, third-, and fourth-year student—an incredible achievement. We hope that Ōishi will be back too, as his kendo was so orthodox and strong. *Kendo World* will of course be at the 65th AJKC in November 2017. As always, we film the matches every year, and you can check them out on our YouTube channel. Also, we will be visiting the 8-dan championships in April 2017, so please keep a look out for our videos from that competition, too.

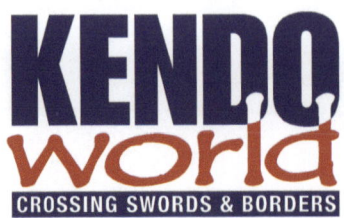

PUBLICATIONS

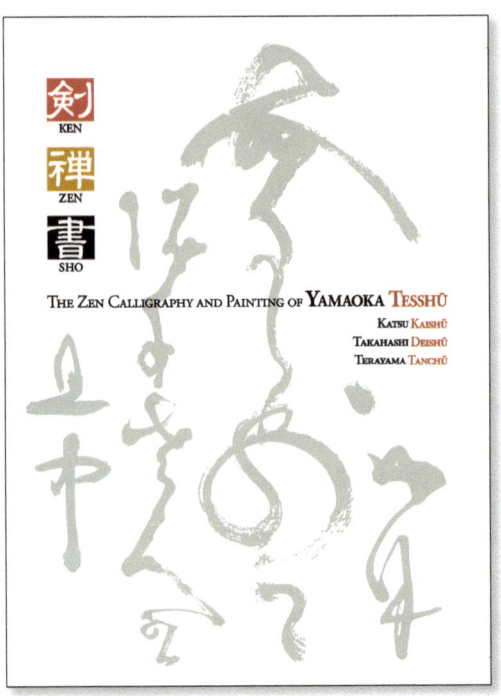

Ken Zen Sho
The Zen Calligraphy and Painting of Yamaoka Tesshu

Yamaoka Tesshu (1836-1888) was a Japanese master of the sword, Zen and calligraphy. This full-colour book on the Zen art of Yamaoka Tesshu features reproductions of extremely valuable calligraphy pieces, and also a number of essays about the relationship between swordsmanship, the study of Zen, and calligraphy. Each one of the works presented is translated into English, and its significance explained in detailed captions. Some fantastic specimens of Zen calligraphy by Tesshu's famous contemporaries Katsu Kaishu and Takahashi Deishu (Tesshu's brother-in-law), and modern master Terayama Tanchu are also featured.

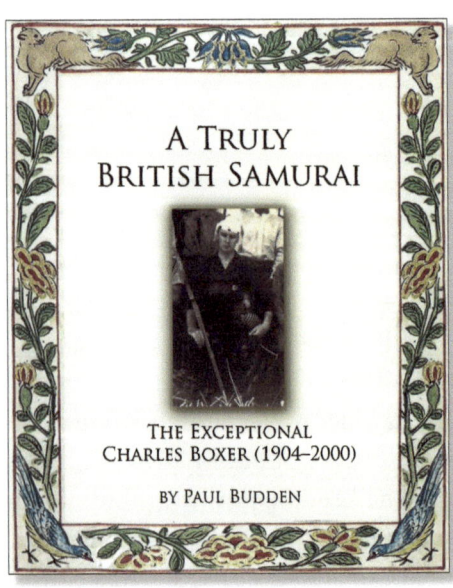

A Truly British Samurai
The Exceptional Charles Boxer

Budo Perspectives

Kendo:
Approaches for all Levels

More info → www.kendo-world.com

Kendo as Music; Music as Kendo

By J. Michael Sills

Let me say first that I'm humbled every day by both kendo and music. The more I practise these arts, the more I realise that what I don't know or understand far outweighs what I do. This piece is about kendo and its relationship to music, and the connections and parallels I've been noticing.

First is how much kendo looks like a dance when two kendoka are engaged in *ji-geiko*. One pushes forward and the other steps back, and then vice versa. Sometimes, they are so synchronised that it can look choreographed—like a dance.

I started playing the guitar at age 12. Rhythm was difficult for me so I studied it in depth. Rhythm is like the *ashi-sabaki* of music: It is the foundation. Later, I submerged myself in the Chicago blues music scene for several years. There were also quite a few highly talented Japanese blues players (Shun Kikuta comes to mind). Blues is made of pure rhythm and 'soul', and to me, *ki* is the kendo equivalent of soul. How hard am I trying? How much am I putting into it? We could go through the motions of *kihon-waza* with a weak *kiai* as *kakarite*, or as *motodachi* just as a blank receiving pad with no real intention. But if soul is missing, what's the point?

Take a song I've played 1,000 times. Can I still give that old song life, soul and intention? I heard one high-level bass player say, "If you don't feel it, don't play it!" This concept seems to relate to both music and kendo. When we do *suburi*, are we just swinging a stick? Or, are we really cutting with intention every single time?

Once, in the middle of a set I was playing on stage, Killer Ray Allison, an elite drummer, sat in for a couple of tunes. About a minute into the next song, sweat began to stream down my face. I wasn't moving any more than I had been, but Killer Ray brought intense *ki* to the stage – it changed everything. When we do kendo with higher-level kendoka, our intensity automatically increases, but when we do *kata* or *kihon*, we can sometimes lose full *ki*. At the end of the 10 kendo *kata*, are we sweating as much as after doing keiko for 10 minutes? Was there *ki* in the *kata*, too? It seems to take great personal discipline to keep a high level of *ki*—especially in situations of a less intense nature.

Even if the music venue that I'm performing at doesn't have a big audience, I still try to dig deep and push out as much energy as I can muster. This is better for the audience, the other musicians, and me as well.

Music has helped my kendo from the aspect of rhythm, especially. We don't really learn to fight in kendo. To me, what we're really learning is how to read our opponent's intentions. If we can do that, the battle is half won—as it will be if we can ascertain their rhythm. I've noticed that a person's *kamae* seems to have some kind of a rhythm to it, something I'll expand upon below. Therefore, if we can come to understand not only our opponent's intention, but also their rhythm, we'll surely be in a good position to score *ippon*.

Here, I need to state some technical aspects of rhythm from a purely musical point of view. Please bear with me. The majority of music that we hear is in 4/4 time. This means that there are 4 beats per measure. But what do we measure? We measure time.

We can vary from a slow tempo to a fast tempo, but in 4/4 time, there are always 4 beats per measure. Therefore, we end up counting time as: 1-2-3-4, 1-2-3-4, over and over. These are referred to as 'quarter notes'. From there, we can sub-divide the time in half. Then, it becomes 1 & 2 & 3 & 4 &. This makes twice as many notes in the same amount of time, and these are referred to as "eighth notes". If we play only the "&s" (or up-beats) and no down-beats (1-2-3-4), we have what is called syncopation. This is syncopation in its most basic form and it is the basis for almost all reggae music. 1 chuck 2 chuck 3 chuck 4 chuck – only playing the chucks. From there, syncopated rhythms can go on to unending complexities.

If a time signature is in 3/4 time, there are 3 beats per measure. Almost all waltz music is in 3/4 time: Oom pa pa, oom pa pa; or 1-2-3, 1-2-3. Most people don't seem to naturally have 3/4 timing in their *kamae*'s rhythm, but it seems though, as noted above, that every person's *kamae* has a kind of rhythm. Let us agree that 1 beat (=) 1 second, so 1 measure (=) 4 seconds.

As it is related to music, rhythm, and kendo, syncopa-

tion seems to be of importance. It is interesting that the rhythm of most people's *kamae* is in 2/4 or 4/4 time, just like most popular music. What I mean by the "rhythm of *kamae*" is, *ashi-sabaki* while in *kamae* can be: 1 front-step 2; and then, 1 back-step 2 in 2/4 time; or 1 front-step 2-3-4, and then 1 back-step 2-3-4 in 4/4 time. So, after evaluating our opponent's rhythm, we can try to strike on the up-beats of

"eighth notes" like: 1-2-3 AND 4; or, 1-2 AND 3-4. Also, switching the feel of our own *kamae* to a 3/4 time seems to sometimes gain an advantage when opposing a 2/4 or 4/4 *kamae* rhythm. This becomes what is called a "polyrhythm" (3s over 4s in this case), which can be difficult for the opponent to understand and therefore difficult to score against.

When doing *keiko* with higher level or fast opponents, we can try to understand (intuitively feel) more of a 1/16 note syncopated timing (1E&A, 2E&A, 3E&A, 4E&A), where (=) 16 notes per 4 beat measure. This is because the duration of openings to strike comes in much shorter intervals with high-level kendoka. This is due to advanced practitioners having such great concentration, which they can sustain for long periods of time. At the same time, the infrequent moments of lapsed concentration become much shorter in duration. To "play" with 7-dan and 8-dan sensei, we may need to understand (intuitively feel) 1/32 note syncopation (32 notes per 4 beat measure) to try to get through their unyielding concentration and mental pressure. Or, just get lucky with our timing now and then… hopefully.

The openings (with high-level kendoka) are very infrequent and short in duration; and therefore highly difficult to anticipate. 1/32 of a 4 beat measure is a small sliver of time—only about 1/8 of a second (remembering our 1 beat (=) 1 second rule). Comparatively, a beginner's vulnerable moments can be for 1 whole beat, or sometimes, they will be open for a whole 4-beat measure.

Music has not just helped my kendo; the opposite is also true. *Kiai* has helped strengthen my voice and given it endurance, which is very important in blues music. Also, when playing marathon sets of four or five hours, I find the state of mind to be similar to that of kendo. It's all about keeping concentration and not losing focus, but also being relaxed and in the moment, all at the same time, so that mental endurance can last all night long.

Kendo has also helped my music with regard to awareness. On stage, especially if I am the band leader, it is very important to monitor the audience, their reactions to the music, body language, etc., while holding the band together in a room full of people. During *keiko*, I try to monitor everyone else in the dojo while enjoying my own *ji-geiko*, but I find it very difficult, especially if my opponent keeps hitting my *men*.

A lot of the older blues cats in Chicago reminded me of kendo sensei in many ways. They were highly sensitive and aware, but with varying degrees of sternness. Some were very kind and some were very strict. But they all seemed to see everything on many levels and not miss much going on musically or otherwise.

Kendo, like music, truly is an art form. In that sense, anything that can be done to increase one's creativity should be pursued. Real creativity can be very fickle, so when it comes, we should try to monitor what may have brought it on and try to repeat the processes that may have triggered it.

In closing, I would like to say that kendo and music have both greatly enriched my life, even if they have both put me through the ringer from time to time. Kendo and music alike seem to have many, possibly infinite, layers and gradations of a physical, emotional and spiritual nature. I have learned that a *kamae* without feeling and intention behind it is only a form. Without feeling and intention behind it, a piece of music is just notes on a page, or sounds in the air.

I hope that we can share in some *keiko* and music, someday.

Uncle Kotay's Kendo Korner

Part 3: The Three Initiatives

Q: Uncle Kotay, as you possess a savant-like knowledge of kendo, I was wondering if you'd be able to help me out. At the dojo the other night I was fighting a gnarly old sensei who was at least three times my age. I thought, as I was a lot younger, stronger, and faster than him, I'd be able to do well. However, after having all my attacks countered, blocked and snuffed out, and my men, kote and doh being peppered with hits, as well as my throat ending up on the pointy end of his shinai, I was mentally and physically spent! I didn't manage to land even one strike. When keiko finished and I went over to him to get some advice, all he said to me was: "Sen wo totte ne." What on earth was he going on about? (#What-the-hell-does-sen-mean?)

A: Well, my young Padawan, he was quite simply telling you to "take the initiative". That is the meaning of "*sen wo toru*"; a very important concept in kendo, and other martial arts, too. Judging from what you have said about your *keiko* with him, it seems that you did not do it once. If you want to be successful in kendo and climb the *dan* ladder, you'll need to be able to take the initiative. Listen carefully while I drop some knowledge. "*Sen*" means "initiative", of which there are three main types that are discussed in kendo. These are "*sen-no-sen*", "*sen-sen-no-sen*", and "*go-no-sen*". Generally speaking, *shikake-waza* are *sen-no-sen* and *sen-sen-no-sen*; *ōji-waza* are *go-no-sen*. Let's take a look at each one.

先の先. *Sen-no-sen* is attacking at the same time as your opponent. You have to look for the moment that their *kamae* breaks as they start to execute a technique and strike the opening. *Debana-kote* is a good example of this.

先々の先. *Sen-sen-no-sen* is the most difficult of the three types but the one that will earn you the most kudos if you're able to do it successfully. When facing your opponent, look for any subtle changes in their *kamae* or demeanour. It's almost as if you're sensing when they are about to attack. When you think that they are, attack before they do, effectively snuffing out their technique before it's even begun. But be careful: they will probably be on the lookout for the same signals coming from you! Techniques that utilise *sen-sen-no-sen* are *osae-waza* or *harai-waza*.

後の先. *Go-no-sen* is where you allow your opponent to make a strike, which you counter. For example, if your opponent tries to strike your *men*, at the moment their technique is almost complete and they are wholly committed, counter. Do not pre-empt or snuff out their technique as in *sen-no-sen* or *sen-sen-no-sen*. Examples of this are *ōji-waza* like *men-suriage-men*, *men-kaeshi-dō*, and *men-nuki-dō*.

Here's a really useful tip to help you come to understand *sen-no-sen* and *sen-sen-no-sen* opportunities and timings. The next time you are *motodachi* in *kihon* practice, as soon as you see the *kakarite* start to move when making a strike, move your right foot forward just a fraction. Do not strike or counterattack; let the *kakarite* strike you. But do not stand there like a striking dummy - make the most of the situation. Eventually, after lots of practice, you will start to see the moment that your opponent is going to strike, and with more practice you'll be able to act upon that opportunity. Of course, it's not possible to do *sen-no-sen*, *sen-sen-no-sen*, or *go-no-sen* without strong *seme*, or pressure. But that's a conversation for another day. So, unless you want to end up kebab-like on the end of your sensei's *shinai*, think about what I've told you today and try to apply it the next time that you're in the dojo.

The Philosophy of MIYAMOTO MUSASHI'S GORIN-NO-SHO

UOZUMI Takashi
(originally appeared in *iichiko intercultural* journal, Autumn 2011.)
Translation by Jeff Broderick

Kuyō Tomoe (Jewel-shaped Navagraha), Musashi's *kamon*.

UOZUMI Takashi: Born 1953. Graduated from Tokyo University, Department of Arts and Humanities, with a PhD in Literature. Former Professor at International Budo University, now at Open University of Japan. Principal works include *Miyamoto Musashi—The Path of the Japanese* (Pelican), *The Annotated Gorin-no-sho* (Shinjinbutsu Oraisha), *Miyamoto Musashi—Living the Martial Path* (Iwanami Shinsho), *Evaluating the Bushido of Samurai During the Age of Warfare* (Shinjinbutsu Oraisha), *Basho's Last Lines* (Chikuma Sensho), and others.

Although Miyamoto Musashi is extremely famous as a swordsman, for a long time, details of his actual life were not well known. It would also be very difficult to say that the aim and overall meaning of his *Gorin-no-sho* has been well understood. I have been working to shed light on Musashi's ideology by examining five of his writings and his *Gorin-no-sho*, along with a re-examination of various materials from the Edo period that capture the true figure of Musashi in the historical context of that era. Previously, I have authored *Miyamoto Musashi—The Path of the Japanese* (2002), *The Annotated Gorin-no-sho* (2005), and *Miyamoto Musashi: Living the Martial Path* (2008). Building on these works, I would like to consider here Musashi's philosophy based on his life and experiences and also his aims in writing the *Gorin-no-sho*.

The Intentions of *Gorin-no-sho*

Why did Musashi write *Gorin-no-sho*?[1] If we wish to understand this work, we should determine his reasons for writing it. Musashi makes this clear from the outset:

> "After many years of training, I have decided to write down my thoughts concerning my martial path, which I have called *Niten Ichi-ryū*. Now, at the start of October in the tenth year of Kan'ei [1645], in the land of Higo in Kyushu [Kumamoto], I climb Mount Iwato and pray to the Heavens, pay my respects to Kannon, and face Buddha. I am a warrior of Harima, Shinmen Musashi no kami Fujiwara Genshin, 60 years of age."[2]

Although he writes "many years of training", Musashi has spent his entire life disciplining himself on the martial path (*hyōhō no michi*). He refers to himself as "a warrior of Harima". It seems that he was born around Tenshō 10 (1582) near Honnō-ji in Harima, but some background: his clan fought on the losing side against Oda Nobunaga and subsequently, under Toyotomi Hideyoshi's policy of separation of warriors and peasants, he stayed with the Shinmen family in Mimasaka until age 9 as an adopted child of Shinmen Munisai[3]. Some sixty years later, increasingly conscious that his death could not be far off, Musashi turned to the transcendental— "the heavens" and "Kannon" — and wrote in an earnest attempt to grasp the truths of existence. "Without quoting Buddhist scripture or the proverbs of Confucius, nor using the old war tales or military writings, I express the true spirit of this school." Musashi does not make use of the Buddhist or Confucian thinking so dominant at the time, nor does he draw upon historical documents such as military classics or war records. Instead he uses his own words and his own experiences from a life spent following the "martial way" to write down its "true spirit".

Musashi states that his reason for wanting to leave this written record is his belief that "Now, there are surely no *bushi* in the world who understand the way of *hyōhō* (tactics)." With the exception of the Shimabara uprising, 30 years of peace had passed since the siege of Osaka castle, and young warriors had grown up accustomed to Tokugawa rule, not knowing actual battle. Not only that, they did not know what it was to risk one's life in mortal combat. "They adorn the martial arts with unnecessary colour and flowery decoration, making a pretence at technique, speaking of this dojo or that dojo"— teaching knowledge which has not been acquired through actual combat. "Half-baked martial arts are a source of grievous wounds," he writes, meaning that a little knowledge is a dangerous thing. "To know even a small part of the art of *kenjutsu* is very difficult." Musashi wants to pass on knowledge of the true martial path to future generations of warriors, and this is his mindset as he sets out to write the *Gorin-no-sho*.

In fact, three years prior to writing *Gorin-no-sho*, Musashi wrote his *Thirty-five Articles of Strategy* for his patron, lord of the Kumamoto domain, Hosokawa Tadatoshi[4]. Tadatoshi was already a *menkyo-kaiden* of Shinkage-ryū, having been conferred a copy of the *Heihō-kadensho* from Yagyū Munenori himself. Musashi offered his work as a treatise of his own two-sword style of swordsmanship. At that time, he wanted to express his explanations in terms that would be understood even by proponents of other styles. This work was a technical manual submitted to the lord only, with the assumption that any questions he had would be answered later. Unfortunately, Lord Tadatoshi passed away a month after receiving the document.

Gorin-no-sho was a further attempt, two and a half years later, to leave an explanation of the way of strategy for future generations of warriors to bear in mind. Based upon his writings in *Thirty-five Articles of Strategy,* it is a further expansion of his ideas on

In the chūdan posture, one of five basic kamae in Niten Ichi-ryū, both swords are held outstretched at roughly shoulder-height.

Past Sōke of Niten Ichi-ryū, Iwami Toshio-sensei demonstrates hidari-wakigamae.

how warriors should live their lives.

Musashi's Experiences Leading to *Gorin-no-sho*

Gorin-no-sho is based on Musashi's experiences disciplining himself and training in the martial arts, so let me first outline those experiences. Musashi writes that, from a young age, having set his heart on following the martial path, he had his first duel and victory at age 13. Although not explicit in his writing, from a young age Musashi had trained under his adoptive father Miyamoto Muni, a famous warrior renowned as *Tenka Musō* (unmatched under heaven), in Muni's Tōri-ryū.[5]

In particular, two years after the Battle of Sekigahara, Musashi went to Kyoto and his *musha shugyō* (warrior training, i.e., travelling and participating in duels) began in earnest. After defeating the famed Yoshioka Ichimon, Musashi defeated a large group of his pupils and took on the title of *Tenka Ichi* (singular under heaven, or number one under heaven).[6] The next year, in Keichō 10 (1605) Musashi established the Enmei-ryū with the creation of his 28-article work, *Heidōkyō* (Mirror of the Martial Way).[7]

After this, in Edo, around Kyoto, and throughout Kyushu, Musashi won numerous duels, finally defeating Kojirō at Ganryū Island. The well-known story, "The Duel on Ganryū Island" is a fictional account based on the *Nitenki*, a record made some 130 years after Musashi's passing.[8] According to the monument in Kokura erected five years after his death, "Both men met at the same time" on the uninhabited Ganryū Island, Musashi facing Kojirō's 3-*shaku* longsword with his 4-*shaku* wooden sword. With a single blow, victory was Musashi's.[9]

Musashi used both swords to his advantage. One technique was to trap the opponent's sword in a scissor-type block.

The migi-wakigamae of Niten Ichi-ryū. The short sword is held out while the long sword stands at the ready on the right hip.

In the *Gorin-no-sho*, Musashi does not mention the above matters, writing only that from the age of 13 until 28 or 29, he "travelled from land to land, facing swordsmen from many different schools, and fighting over 60 duels without once being defeated." Whatever the case, he put his life on the line in over 60 duels where he faced opponents who were every bit as committed to victory as he was, and beat them all, proof that he deserved the title of "Best Swordsman Under Heaven".

After reaching age 30, however, Musashi looked back at his past victories and, realising that they had been attained "without the deepest level of *hyōhō*", he began to pursue a "deeper reason". He started to become not simply a warrior, but rather a thinker in search of a broader truth. While continuing his maxim of "train in the morning, practise in the evening" he writes, "I followed my own natural path, and at 50, attained it … From this point forward, I live with no need to pursue this path further." In other words, the truth he found is the ultimate one.

Although not written here, at the time of the Battle of Sekigahara, 19-year-old Musashi was in Kyushu as part of the eastern army under the command of Kuroda Kambei Yoshitaka (Josui), participating in the battle and castle siege of Ishigakibara (1600). At 34, he served in the cavalry under Mizuno Katsunari at the Siege of Osaka (1614), fighting on the side of the Tokugawa, and at age 57, he fought to quell the Shimabara Uprising (1637-1638) along with his adopted son Iori, who was appointed a

shogunal military administrator under Ogasawara Tadamasa.[10] From age 36, Musashi was a guest of the Honda clan in Himeji, and from age 45 was hosted in Akashi by the Ogasawara clan; the clan was later transferred to Kokura by shogunal decree when Musashi was 51. From age 59, Musashi was hosted in Kumamoto as a guest of Lord Hosokawa.[11] At the time he attained mastery of his martial way, around age 50, it is believed that Musashi was helping his son Iori with the legal governance of the realm.[12] All of these experiences form the backdrop for his writing of *Gorin-no-sho*.

The Five Scrolls Comprising *Gorin-no-sho*

Gorin-no-sho consists of five scrolls: Earth, Water, Fire, Air, and Emptiness*. The "Earth Scroll" begins with a preface concerning Musashi's career, then the main body of the text stipulates *hyōhō* as "the way of the warrior." After stating that it concerns both generals and common soldiers alike, it posits the way of *hyōhō* in societal terms, finally describing how to go about learning this path.

The "Water Scroll" begins with a discussion about *kenjutsu* techniques that warriors should understand, such as *kamae* (stances) and the logic of sword usage. It then goes into practical matters concerning technique. These writings summarise his prior technical explanations.

In the "Fire Scroll" Musashi tells how the explanations he gave concerning *kenjutsu* apply not only to a fight with a single adversary, but can be extended to mass battles between thousands or tens of thousands of people.

In the "Wind Scroll" Musashi discusses the failings of other styles of swordsmanship, and sets about showing the correctness of his own teachings.

The "Emptiness Scroll" describes training and

---

* This is written with the *kanji* 空 which means "sky" or more broadly, the heavens, but may also be interpreted to mean "emptiness" or "void".

moreover, the emptiness which one must find in one's heart, as well as the state of openness which is found within that emptiness.

Although a description of *kenjutsu* forms the core of the "Water Scroll" and "Fire Scroll", the *Gorin-no-sho* as a whole is meant to encompass not only *kenjutsu* but the entirety of *hyōhō*. With this in mind, the work is divided into five parts, and the contents of each section are announced in the preface in the "Earth Scroll".[13]

The Content of *Gorin-no-sho*

The "Earth Scroll": The Way of *Hyōhō*

Musashi, in looking broadly at the world, defines the purview of the way of strategy. Medieval Japanese society was divided into four social levels of samurai, farmers, craftsmen, and merchants. Each class had defined jobs. Just as the farmers produced crops, builders constructed dwellings, and merchants conducted trade, the samurai class had to "make ready the tools of war, to know their various advantages; this is the work of the warrior". The meaning of this is that *bushi*, as warriors, were expected to train themselves at all times in preparation for battle. Musashi regards people of all levels without a sense of judgement as to their relative worth, but calmly views their innate abilities. Samurai of this time had already become administrative officials, but without overtly going into this matter, Musashi places samurai firmly in their original role of combatants.

Bushi ranged from general to foot soldier, and Musashi likens this to the ranks of carpenter ranging from master craftsman to common labourer. Like the master carpenter knows how to construct ornate temple buildings, palaces, and multi-storey buildings, the general understands how to exert power in order to rule his household and his domain; he assesses his vassals and determines what they are and are not capable of, like a carpenter chooses suitable uses and placements for different quality materials. Foot soldiers, like the apprentices who keep the tools sharp so that every job may be completed with precision, had to train

"When the enemy makes ready to strike, and you also think to attack, your body becomes the striking body; your heart becomes the striking heart; your hands move strongly and in an instant, without showing your intention to attack." (**The Water Scroll**)

regularly to keep their martial techniques sharp. And these apprentices, by honing their techniques and learning construction methods, could someday reach the rank of master carpenter. Although it was not possible to openly say as much in light of the rigidly stratified society put in place by the *bakufu*, the possibility of "low overthrowing high"—that is, a low-ranking samurai attaining high status with enough talent—may be seen as an appealing loophole from the viewpoint of a warring-states period samurai.

"The path of *hyōhō* that a *bushi* takes is based on surpassing others in all things, whether it is achieving victory in single combat, or in a battle between many; for the advancement of one's lord, or for one's own advancement, seeking to make a name for oneself: this is the path of *hyōhō*." Musashi states that gaining renown through military exploits and victory in battle is the path to success in life, showing that his thinking is very much that of a traditional warrior.

For Musashi, a warrior had to understand the use of all weapons, not just the sword, but spears, *naginata* (halberds), bows, firearms, and more. All must be understood in terms of their strengths and weaknesses, and when and where they should be utilised. Through an understanding of *kenjutsu* and the sword which is always at his side, a warrior can grasp the means to achieve victory in a battle of a thousand or ten thousand men.

The reason for using two swords is that, in a pitched battle to the death, a warrior should use every last weapon available to him, whether he is on horseback, or holding a bow or a spear in one hand; whether the battlefield is muddy, or rocky; whether he is on a narrow path or in a throng of people, he will often need to use a sword one-handed. By practising with two swords, one becomes accustomed to swinging a sword with one hand, and when necessary, wielding one sword with both hands.

Since any kind of situation could arise in battle, Musashi seeks a truth which is applicable at any time. Specific techniques that are only useful in certain situations can be dangerous. Training in *kenjutsu* was necessary for *bushi*, but it was also applicable to artistic pursuits as well. Musashi wrote, "While I have dedicated myself to training in *hyōhō*, when I have tried my hand at the arts, I have done everything without a teacher." In fact, Musashi studied Zen, was proficient in *renga* (linked verse) and the tea ceremony, and a number of his famous works of calligraphy and ink wash painting still survive. Drawing on his own experiences, he explains the path of *hyōhō* in terms of other arts, such as dancing, *kemari* (an ancient form of football), and acrobatics, all of which, like swordsmanship, make use of timing and *metsuke* (gaze). Basing his ideas on an explanation of swordsmanship, Musashi wrote *Gorin-no-sho* as a guide to how samurai should live their lives, via battle, as warriors; thus it may be said that this work is a treatise on *bushido*.[14]

This is the end of Part 1. The second and final part of this article will appear in the next edition of Kendo World.

Endnotes

1. No manuscript of *Gorin-no-sho* exists in Musashi's hand, but for an explanation of why it is certain that it was written by Musashi, see my *Miyamoto Musashi—The Path of the Japanese* (Pelican).
2. Henceforth, quotes from *Gorin-no-sho* are taken from the author's *Annotated Gorin-no-sho* (Shinjinbutsu Oraisha); for the sake of readability, *kanji*, *furigana*, and/or *okurigana* have been added as appropriate. Also, when Musashi writes "pay my respects to Kannon" he means the sacred area dedicated to Kannon at Reigan-ji temple on Mount Iwato.
3. Musashi writes that he is 60 years of age, which would put his birthdate in Tenshō 12 (1584), however it is likely that he means he is "in his sixties." Compatibility with *A Genealogy of the Miyamoto Family* left by his adopted son Iori, as well as other historical evidence suggests that he was born in Tenshō 10 (1582). (See above sources.)
4. *Thirty-five Articles of Strategy* was presented to Lord Hosokawa Tadatoshi, under whose patronage Musashi was staying as a guest, in February of Kan'ei 18 (1641). It is an explanation of the principles of his martial style. Reprinted in above sources.
5. Miyamoto Munisai penned the *Tōri-ryū Mokuroku* ("A curriculum of Tōri-ryū") in Keichō 3 (1598) and signed it "Founded: *Tenka Musō*". The use of "Founded" expresses that it was the first two-sword school. *Tenka Musō* may relate to the title of *Hinoshita Musō* (unmatched under the sun) that Munisai was awarded after winning two matches out of three in front of Shogun Ashikaga Yoshiteru against the Shogunal family fencing instructor Yoshioka Kenbō; this incident is related in the *Kokura Hibun* (a monument erected by Miyamoto Iori). That a young Musashi was thrown out of his home after criticizing his father's *jutte-jutsu* is a fiction based on the *Bushūkōdenrai* written 70 years after Musashi's death.
6. Musashi's reason for challenging Yoshioka Ichimon may have been his father's previous victory in which Munisai received the title of *Tenka Musō*. Details of how the best-of-three challenge was conducted are recorded on the *Kokura Hibun* monument (properly, *Musashi Kenshōhi*).
7. The *Heidōkyō* is signed by Miyamoto Musashi-no-Kami Fujiwara no Gikei; this appears to be the name adopted by the young Musashi. It can be found on copies given to early students and on four related documents. The postscript is dated "Winter of Keichō 9", denoted "In past and present, peerless martial art" and signed "Enmei-ryū Tenka Ichi". It seems to be intended as a private or secret document. In the document, terminology from Musashi's father Munisai's *Tōri-ryū Mokuroku* may be seen throughout. (For a detailed examination, see above sources.)
8. Concerning The Duel on Ganryū Island, some eighty years after Musashi's death, a number of stories emerged after a kabuki play entitled *Katakiuchi Ganryūjima* ("Revenge on Ganryū Island") gained fame in the three large cities of Kyoto, Osaka, and Edo. The *Nitenki* incorporated a number of these stories. After the writing of *Miyamoto Musashi* (1935—1939) by novelist Yoshikawa Eiji, numerous movies, plays, radio dramas, and comic strips were produced, repeating the story and adding to its renown.
9. In his later years, Musashi gave the long wooden sword he carved and used in this duel to a chief retainer of the Kumamoto domain, Nagaoka Yoriyuki. It measures 4-*shaku* 2-*sun* 5-*bu* (126.8 cm). (In the holdings of the Matsui Museum Collection.)
10. No extant materials prove Musashi's whereabouts at the time of the Battle of Sekigahara, but his adoptive father Muni was already in the employ of the Kuroda-*han* at this time, according to the Kuroda family record *Bushūkōdenrai*. As for the Osaka campaign and the Shimabara uprising, Musashi's name appears in the military rosters of the Mizuno clan and the Ogasawara clan.
11. After the Siege of Osaka, Musashi lived in Himeji near his familial home, as a guest—not a retainer—of the Honda clan, who had been put in control of Himeji following the ousting of the Ikeda family. Musashi was said to be a guest of the daimyo, employed as a fencing instructor to the domain swordsmen.
12. Iori was Musashi's nephew, second son of his older brother. Upon being adopted by Musashi, he entered the service of the Akashi Ogasawara clan, and five years later was made a minister of the daimyo, a position of great prestige. This exceptional career advancement is thought to have come about with the assistance of his father, who used his knowledge of the local area to help Iori with civil planning; this was in addition to Musashi's numerous contributions and fine reputation. A year later, the clan was transferred to Kokura in Kyushu, where Iori's conspicuous efforts, along with his service in the Shimabara rebellion, was noted and he was made head minister.
13. A year and a half after starting to write, and a week before his death, Musashi gave a copy of *Gorin-no-sho* to his direct disciple Terao Magonojō on May 12, in Tempo 2 (1645). Musashi, suffering from a long illness, was not able to provide him with a final draft, but as Magonojō writes in the inscription dated Keian 4 (1651), Musashi did finish writing the full contents.
14. It is a treatment of *bushido* in the sense that it discusses how a *bushi* should live his life. The term *bushido* had been used from the end of the Warring States Period to the start of the Edo Period in military histories such as the *Kōyō-gunkan* and *Shoka hyōtei*. While Musashi uses the phrase "the path/way of *hyōhō*" he clearly means the way of life for the *bushi*. While war was almost unthinkable in the midst of the era of peace, Musashi's work differs from *Hagakure* and other works concerning *bushido* appearing 70 years later, in that it was not written as a warning to samurai. Furthermore, this *bushido* has nothing to do with the ideology of the same name which became prominent in the Meiji Period.

KENDO FOR ADULTS

By Hatano Toshio (Courtesy of *Kendo Nihon*)
Translated by Alex Bennett

Hatano Toshio-sensei was born in January 1945 in Musashi Murayama, Tokyo. After graduating from Kokushikan High School and Nihon University, he became a salaryman for a few years before establishing the Nanbudō Kendōgu shop in 1971. He passed the 8-dan exam on his second attempt in 1994. He serves as an advisor for the West Tokyo Kendo Federation, and is Suruga University Kendo Club Shihan, Musashi Murayama City Kendo Federation president, and leader of the Kinryūkan Dojo.

Part 5: The Importance of Kakari-geiko for Adults

There are two objectives in *kakari-geiko*: the first is building stamina, especially in school-aged kenshi; the second is to learn to strike without using excessive strength. The latter is the most important reason. When you are completely exhausted and have little strength left in your arms and shoulders, this is when you make the best cuts because you are striking with a minimum amount of power. You need to remember this feeling. Striving to maintain correct posture and form as you go will help perfect your striking, and lead to executing attacks that are relaxed, accurate, and decisive. Start energetically, and finish energetically. That is the only way to do *kakari-geiko*.

Kakari-geiko should not be done for excessively long stretches. It is more effective to do short spirited spurts with rest intervals in-between. Adults may not be able to attend training as much as they would like, so it is essential that *kakari-geiko* is done in a way to glean the most benefit in the limited time available.

It is easy to tell if somebody has been raised on a staple diet of *kakari-geiko*. Their movement will be fluid and their *kamae* will be watertight but relaxed. This is proof that they have developed a style of kendo through *kakari-geiko* that is not based on strength, but rather by not using strength. Although adults will no longer possess the same athletic prowess and physical resilience of their younger days, it is important that they undertake *kakari-geiko* whenever possible.

Motodachi skill is crucial in *kakari-geiko*. It is very difficult for the attacker to strike correctly if the spatial distance is too great. *Motodachi* must constantly manoeuvre to the one-step one-strike interval. This will encourage the attacker to keep striking steadily without interruption. When receiving for children, it is a good idea to keep telling them what targets to strike next. "*Kote*, next'll be *hiki-dō…*" This will make the *kakari-geiko* session flow smoothly. If a kid has a habit of petering out after the strike, you can give them a little push with your *shinai* and get them used to following through.

The ideal strike is made when you have no more strength left

With adults who are keen to excel in their kendo, it is effective to nullify or ward off some of their attacks by diverting their *shinai*. It is exhausting when your *shinai* is deflected to the side as you try to go straight through. This is the point as it will develop core strength. At college-level tournaments, a noticeable difference between strong and weak teams or players is in the degree of core strength. Those with inferior core strength, for example, lose their balance easily in *taiatari*. Strong players are always stable and poised because they obviously train very hard and have developed a sturdy foundation.

At Suruga University, where I teach kendo, I sometimes get the students to wrestle with each other. Toward the end of training when they are starting to show fatigue, I make them do *kakari-geiko* followed by grappling. The rules are simple: no grabbing *himo*, and no letting go of *shinai*. Those who are strong in *keiko* always prevail when it comes to wrestling, and the weaker kenshi usually get thrown around like ragdolls as they are unable to lower their hips. It doesn't matter how strong you are physically; if you are unable to lower your hips you will be unable to

Do not let each kakari-geiko round go for too long. Have short breaks between each turn

generate much power. The trick to wrestling, just as in sumo, is to utilise opposite force. If you push from the right to the left, the opponent will respond by pushing back to keep balance. Then, if you respond in turn by pulling them from left to right, they will fall over easily.

Motodachi should "mix it up" by warding off some attacks, dodging, and doing body clashes to give the attacker a full work out

Closing the Gap

I rank the strongest college kenshi in increments of 0.1. The best students fall around the 1.0–1.4 mark. At Suruga University, a few of the club members have competed at the national high school championships in the past, but lost in the early rounds. They would be around 1.5–1.9. Those who only went as far as the regional championships would be in 2.0–2.1 range. I tell my students at Suruga University that the top class of 1.0–1.4 often drop in level when they enter university; whereas, those in the 1.5–1.9 group tend to improve. Eventually they will meet at 1.5, which makes it very competitive.

Although some students are famous for their exploits in their high school days, this is the past. High school and university are different worlds. Competitions are won by the strongest on the day. So, the secret is how strong you are now, not one year ago. But how do you get strong now? The first step is to realise that you are weak. Even if you won some prestigious tournament, forget it. Use the realisation that you are weak as a catalyst to improve by any means possible. Go running, do weight training, and so on to make your *shinai* speed faster. Then you will start seeing the "answers". This applies to kenshi of all ages.

A famous Japanese baseball player named Ichiro is quite remarkable in terms of his all-round ability and record. However, I am sure he never for a moment rests on his laurels. He is always looking to get better, to find that edge. This attitude is important in kendo. You must search for answers, but first you need to ask yourself questions. "I am weak so, what can I do to improve?" is the best place to start. This is where the divide between first-rate and second-rate kenshi becomes evident.

Hatano Masashi's Observation

Morishima Tateo-sensei was always strict on *motodachi* during *kakari-geiko* when I was a student at Meiji University. The *maai* should not be too far or too close, but at the optimal distance for striking. *Motodachi* should have the intention of *seme*—or looking to seize openings in the attacker. He was always quick to remonstrate *motodachi* who weren't thinking about what they were doing. As students, we never really understood what he meant and just blindly did what he said. But now, many years later, I can see the logic behind his teachings.

It's excruciating but,
   endure, persevere,
     the flower will bloom

From Katate Guntō-jutsu to Tanken-jutsu:

The birth of Tankendo

By Baptiste Tavernier

Introduction

In *Kendo World 7.3* we explained how a plague of silkworm diseases in the second half of the 19th century led France to sign the Treaty of Amity and Commerce in October 1858, which marked the official beginning of Franco-Japanese relationships, and how this event indirectly precipitated the agreement on the first French military mission to Japan in June 1866.

Through the successive French military missions, the newly formed Imperial Army was introduced to European fencing, especially sabre (*guntō-jutsu*) and bayonet (*jūken-jutsu*).

Japan's Army Ministry published a military fencing textbook called *Kenjutsu Kyōhan* in 1889 with numerous revisions thereafter. Its first edition was based on translations of French military teaching materials and thus detailed French fencing concepts and techniques. However, from the 2nd edition, Japan moved towards a hybrid system that still used Western concepts (one-handed sword style) but blended with *gekken* (traditional Japanese fencing) methodology: this new system advocated the use of *shinai* and *bōgu* and reverted to a more Japanese style of etiquette (*reigi*).

After the Russo-Japanese War (1905), army authorities judged that *guntō-jutsu* was not effective enough. Another revision of the *Kenjutsu Kyōhan* was thus published in 1907, and a new category of *guntō-*

Graphic 1: Japanese soldiers training in French sabre and bayonet, circa 1887

jutsu was introduced: *bajō guntō-jutsu* or *guntō-jutsu* on horseback. From 1915, the Japanese army decided to discard the one-handed sabre system and to promote instead two-handed *morote guntō-jutsu*, a modified version of kendo for military use. The old *guntō-jutsu* was then renamed *katate guntō-jutsu*, and practised only by cavalry officers.

From 1919, the Japanese army worked on the elaboration of a new one-handed close quarter combat system called *tanken-jutsu*, based on detached bayonet fighting and Japanese *kodachi* techniques. As a result, *katate guntō-jutsu* slowly disappeared as bayonet and detached bayonet techniques became the main curricula before and during World War II.

Tanken-jutsu: the birth of tankendo

The *tanken-jutsu* combat system was first devised and matured at the Toyama Military Acadamy. Its content was then published in 1922 in a textbook entitled *Tanken-jutsu Oyobi Oyō Kenjutsu no Kenkyū* (Research on *tanken-jutsu* and advanced *kenjutsu*).

The 74-page booklet is divided into two main sections: *tanken-jutsu* and advanced *kenjutsu*, although the title of section 2 is misleading since this part deals in fact with *jūken-jutsu* (bayonet fencing) only. The content of "advanced" bayonet fencing is actually very interesting: it details two sets of *kata* that do not exist anymore in modern jukendo. This is beyond the scope of this article, nevertheless I will explain them in a future issue of *Kendo World*.

Back to section 1 and *tanken-jutsu*, which is itself divided into three main chapters: *tanken* vs. *tanken* (detached bayonet confrontation), *tanken* vs. *jūken* (detached bayonet against fixed bayonet), and *tanken* vs. *morote guntō* (detached bayonet against military sabre). Only the *tanken* vs. *tanken* part features photographs where practitioners wear *bōgu*. The rest of the book shows different techniques but in a *kata* fashion.

Those who know or practise modern tankendo will soon notice several differences with the 1922 *tanken-jutsu*. The most striking one is that practitioners wear both *kote*. In tankendo, one only wears the right *kote*, leaving the left hand free for grappling techniques (called *seitai waza*). This indicates that the original *tanken* vs. *tanken* curriculum did not include any grappling phases; and indeed the 1922 textbook does not introduce any *seitai waza* in this chapter. However, close quarter attacks and grappling techniques are featured in the other sections where the *tanken* fights against longer weapons (fixed bayonet or sword).

Another interesting difference is that the left hand is not kept on the hip as it is in modern tankendo, but sways free in the same manner as in *katate guntō-jutsu* (cf. Graphic 2). This is worth mentioning because it clearly shows the shift in the way Japanese sensei thought out post-war tankendo when they reinstated it. At that time it seemed crucial to somehow break away from militaristic influences, and a certain "revisionist" trend started to appear: tankendo was

Graphic 2: *Guntō-jutsu,* a hybrid system that mixes European sabre and Japanese *gekken*.

Graphic 3: *Guntō-jutsu* on horseback
(Kendo World is actually saving money to upkeep two horses and try this. #badasskendo #agincourt #notgoingtoendwell)

advertised as a budo focusing on short sword (i.e. *kodachi*) and not a detached bayonet. Many aspects of tankendo now derive from that trend: the left hand is kept on the hip in order to symbolise the presence of a *saya* in the sash; the use of the same curved *bokutō* that is used in kendo instead of a straight one (the 1922 *kata* were performed with an actual bayonet in hand, or a straight *bokken* with a small *tsuba*); the reconfiguring of some techniques to look more kendo-like, etc. As a side note, the 1922 *tan-shinai* is 1cm shorter than that used now, and measures 52 cm.

1–Basic techniques

The *datotsu-bui* (striking areas) presented in the 1922 textbook are the same as in modern tankendo, with one exception: since practitioners wear both *kote*, one can strike the opponent's left hand as well. *Datotsu-bui* are shown in Graphic 4 (we added the red dots over the original black and white ones, for clarity).

The text explanations in this book are kept very short. *Kihon-dōsa* or "basic technique" is done in

Graphic 4: *shitotsu* (thrust) and *zangeki* (slash) targets

Graphic 5: *kihon-dōsa*; *nodo no tsuki*

Graphic 6: *men harai* followed by *men*
(Yes, the backgrounds don't match)

pairs, with a *motodachi* who acts as instructor, and the student. The manual insists on the importance of *kihon-dōsa* for acquiring correct movements and posture, and advocates that each training session start and end with it. This is actually still the case, although the content of tankendo's *kihon-dōsa* has evolved greatly since 1922. The textbook states the commands that the *motodachi* must shout to the trainee, followed by a succinct description of the technique. Interestingly, the manual does not mention absorption, the small step back peculiar to jukendo and tankendo and performed by the *motodachi* in order to reduce the shock in the students wrists and elbows. Therefore, we are not sure if the concept of absorption was present in 1922, or if it was so evident that they did not feel the need to note it…

The 1922 *kihon-dōsa* sequence is as follow:
—*nodo no tsuki* (Graphic 5).
—*men uchi*.
—*harai* on *nodo no tsuki* followed by a thrust to the *dō*.
—*harai* on *men uchi* (close to a *suri-age*) followed by a *men uchi* (Graphic 6).

2–Advanced techniques

The 1922 manual then jumps straight into advanced

techniques, labelled as "*kihon-dōsa* variations for *shiai*". Interestingly enough, although the left *kote* is a valid target, there isn't a single exercise featuring a strike to it in this book.

The textbook introduces five advanced techniques, some of them featuring different possible final strikes.

a– Stepping aside and striking *men* when the opponent advances or retreats.

b– *Debana* when the opponent raises his *tanken* to strike *men*. The attack can be either *nodo* or *dō tsuki*, or *men* or *kote* strike (Graphic 7).

c– Feint: leaving one's *kote* open for the opponent to strike, and do a *debana nodo*, *dō* or *men* (Graphic 8 & 9).

d– *Suri-age* to an incoming *men* strike while pivoting to the right, followed by a *tsuki* to *nodo* or *dō*.

e– The last technique resembles what aikidoka would call *irimi/tenkan*: to an incoming *tsuki*, the student steps in diagonally to the right while pivoting to dodge the *motodachi*'s attack and strikes back at *dō*, *nodo* or *kote* (Graphic 10).

Tanken vs. longer weapons: the first kata

Parts 2 & 3 of the *tanken-jutsu* section introduce techniques to oppose an enemy armed with *jūken* (fixed bayonet) or *morote guntō* (two-handed military sabre). The book details several techniques but this time in a *kata*-like manner, i.e. practitioners do not wear *bōgu*. Actually the Tanken Tai Mokujū No Kata (*tanken* vs. bayonet) and the Tanken Tai Tō No Kata (*tanken* vs. sword) practised nowadays (cf. *Kendo World 5.3* & *6.1*) have their roots in these techniques.

There is an interesting difference however: in the 1922 manual, it is explained that one can stab or strike *men* when grappling whereas in modern tankendo, a strike to the head in this situation would be disregarded (Graphic 11).

The textbook explains a dozen ways of entering the *maai* and winning against a fixed bayonet, and four techniques to defeat the sabre (Graphic 12), two of them being exactly the same techniques as in the modern *kata*.

Graphic 7: *debana kote* on *furi-age men*

Graphic 8: opening *kote*...

Graphic 9: *debana dō!*

Graphic 10: dodging *tsuki* with *kote* strike

Graphic 11: *men* strike at close quarters

Graphic 12: preemptive grab on a *furi-age men*. This technique made its way into the modern sets of *kata*, albeit not against the sword but as the last technique of the Tankendo No Kata (*tanken* vs *tanken*)

To conclude

The publication of the *tanken-jutsu* textbook in 1922 marks the birth of tankendo. More than a simple curiosity, I believe that studying its content is actually quite beneficial. First, by comparing it to the content of the modern curriculum, one can get a clear insight on how an actual combat system "evolved" into a budo, or "modern martial way". We can examine here techniques that have long been forgotten or banned, and techniques that are still in use nowadays but presented in their original, sometimes unrefined version.

Second, the very fact that this manual describes an actual combat system makes its content, *a priori*, effective. This is especially interesting when it comes to *ishujiai*, i.e. a fight against a jukendo or a kendo exponent. Indeed, there is no longer a dedicated instruction for such situations, except through a limited number of *kata*. Therefore, the techniques explained in this manual are still helpful for the modern practitioner.

Dojo Files

Phnom Penh Kendo Club

Name of Club: Phnom Penh Kendo Club
Year Established: 2009
Venue: Olympic Stadium, Phnom Penh, Cambodia
Number of Members: approx. 25
Weekly Practice Times:
–Tuesdays 6pm-8pm, –Thursdays (iaido) 6pm-8pm, –Saturdays 10am-12pm, –Sundays 10am-12pm
Classes on Offer: kendo, iaido
Instructors:
Osuga-sensei (7-dan) leads the instruction with the aid of Jeff-sensei (4-dan), Yoshida-san (3-dan), and Mori-san (shodan).
What does a typical training session consist of?
Keiko concentrates on the basic foundations of *ashi-sabaki*, *kihon*, *shikake-waza*, and *ōji-waza*, and *ji-geiko*. There is an emphasis on *seme*.
Club Social Media:
www.facebook.com/PPKendoClub/
Club History:
The Phnom Penh Kendo Club was established in 2009 by Victor Aguayo, originally from San Francisco dojo, along with another couple of kendoka. He was the head instructor at that time. Since then, the dojo has been steadily growing. PPKC is currently the only kendo dojo in Cambodia and hosts about 25 members from around the world. It is a very international group of dedicated kendoka.

In December of 2015, a new dojo building was completed. The dojo, located at the Olympic Stadium in Phnom Penh, now hosts kendo, iaido, aikido, and karate. Each room has been specifically designed for the respective arts, with the kendo dojo featuring a sprung floor. Much appreciation goes to Mr. Itaru Mori who championed the dojo construction project.

Currently, Osuga-sensei leads *keiko* with the help of 4-dan, 3-dan and 2-dan kendoka. PPKC was just recently recognised by the Kingdom of Cambodia as a national team due to the dojo's efforts at the All Asean Taikai held in Bangkok, Thailand, in 2016. The dojo continues to grow as more Cambodian and international practitioners accept the lifelong commitment to self improvement through the art of the sword.

All levels, ages, genders and nationalities are welcome to join and practise kendo and iaido at Phnom Penh Kendo Club. We are looking forward to seeing you!

> **shugyō** (n.)
> The process of rigorously training and polishing one's mind and body. See **musha-shugyō**.
>
> (AJKF, *Japanese-English Dictionary of Kendo*)

The Shugyō Mind: Part 3
By Alex Bennett

"Keiko is for learning things you don't know how to do. Always toiling in your comfort zone is not keiko."

Of course, we kenshi repeat the same basic techniques and exercises in *keiko*, constantly revising and polishing skills and techniques we are already proficient at. The point of this adage is to remind kenshi that the real benefits in *keiko* come from venturing outside of one's comfort zone. It goes without saying really, but it's not always that easy. Once you have created your rhythm and style—your comfort zone—it is difficult to break free from the mould.

That is why bad habits often go unfixed, and there is always a degree of trepidation about trying techniques that you are not particularly confident with. It's easier just to stick to what you know because training will be smoother, and you won't make a complete ass out of yourself by missing the timing and target. Make no mistake, however, such an approach to kendo will ultimately stymie development.

I'm sure that many readers have an inkling of what I'm talking about. We all have our favourite techniques, and most of us have a proclivity to stick to what we know. Let's say that you are quite proficient at scoring *debana-kote*. Just as your opponent is about to launch a *men* attack, your body is able to move effortlessly and decisively to pop that *kote* off as if it was the most natural thing in the world.

Dō, on the other hand, may be something that you are not so adept at. You might have a 50/50 success rate in *kihon*, so it is something that you shy away from in *keiko*, let alone *shiai*. Why? There may be several reasons: for example, you are wary that your *men* will get hit first and you will lose, so you'd rather not risk it; or, you are afraid of hitting your training partner painfully in the armpit. So, if you can get away with just doing that super-duper special *debana-kote* technique of yours in training (or competition), that is exactly what you will do. If you must practise *dō* during *keiko*, you will be overly restrained, and noticeably timid with its execution compared to your comfort techniques. *Tsuki* is another *waza* that often gets laid by the wayside, or put in the "too hard basket" for similar reasons. It is understandable, and perhaps your partner might be secretly grateful.

Nevertheless, this is where you must overcome your hesitation and learn to relish the opportunity to work on something that you are, well, crap at doing. Sure, you will hit your partner under the arms, and it will absolutely sting. You will miss the *tsuki-dare* causing the *shinai* to scrape along your partner's neck and give

them the hickey from hell. You will feel awkward, frustrated, and embarrassed at the same time, so what do you do? Avoid it? Or, take the bull by the horns and work at it until you can confidently add another *waza* to your bag of tricks?

That was a rhetorical question, but it actually takes guts to do this, and is precisely why the technical development of many kenshi reaches an impasse. The best kind of kendo is rounded kendo. There are four targets, and you must strive to be able to hit all of them with the same degree of confidence and effectiveness. It won't happen overnight. Actually, it takes years and years, but it will never happen if you don't make an effort.

Remember that the *shinai* is not an axe. Axe blows hurt and can be dangerous, so there is no shame in starting slowly and accurately. Build your confidence in your worst techniques little by little. Striking your partner by accident in un-armoured parts of the body is not ideal, but it happens [a lot] in *keiko*. You will hit, and you will be hit, so there must be mutual understanding. You are working together to improve—that's why *rei* before and after is so important. *Onegai-shimasu* = "Thank you for the opportunity to hone my skills by whacking you as accurately as I can with my *shinai*. Allow me to apologise in advance, and please forgive any wayward strikes that miss the mark." *Arigatō gozaimashita* = "Thank you for that round of *keiko*. I hope that my wayward strikes didn't hurt too much, and I most certainly hold no grudges for the welt(s) you gave me on the side of my head/torso/arm/pride. Onwards and upwards. Cheers mate."

Every now and again, you will come across some enfeebled, highly volatile hypochondriac who insists on making a big song and dance when they cop a painful, albeit unintentional wayward blow. Their intention is to make you feel bad about their excruciating pain, make an appeal about the severe hardships they are forced to endure [because of you], thereby accentuating your ineptitude and their good graces and spirit of self-sacrifice. Screw them! Get over it. Suck it up. No pain no gain. Battle scars are proof of hard training, and should be laughed off as just another one of life's unfair lessons. I can't remember the number of cracked ribs, burst eardrums, *sakura* imprints on my throat, kiss marks on my neck, and bruises from head to toe in my 30 years of kendo. And, although not proud of the fact, I have certainly inflicted as much as I have received as a result of my own lack of proficiency. Most of the time you don't even notice until you are having a shower.

Another related aspect in kendo is to seek out training partners who you feel very uncomfortable fighting. This may include opponents who are physically domineering, really fast, quirky beyond belief, rude, short, tall, old, young, uncoordinated, or just plain scary. There is a tendency to avoid opponents who are going to make your *keiko* life less than enjoyable for one reason or another, and we justify it to ourselves with all manner of lily-livered excuses. "I'll tackle him tomorrow", "I don't get anything out of training with him/her", "His kendo is just too weird", "All she is worried about is getting points so the *keiko* is 'pointless'", "He hurts too much…"

Let's face it, the real reason behind any reluctance to engage certain people or types of kendo is because your kendo doesn't work against it. Again, it is easier to fight a person who you get on with, and who doesn't take you too far from your comfort zone. That is, people who you have a fighting chance against, or maybe a famous sensei who rips you apart, but at least you can brag that you've "been there". This is nothing more than "disingenuous-*keiko*", and apart from being insolent, superficial, and most un-budo-like, you are only fooling yourself. Next time you notice these thoughts crossing your mind during *keiko*, ask yourself why. You might just find that it's not a problem with your opponent, but more so an issue with your own failures.

As with making an effort to master the techniques you just can't get your head around, the same can be said of opponents who you would rather not cross swords with if you had a choice. The more people you fight, the more styles of kendo you have to deal with—the good, the bad, and the ugly—the more rounded your kendo will become. This is true *keiko*, and what *shugyō* is all about.

REI DAN JI CHI

The Greater Meaning of Kendo

Reidan-jichi Part 22
Various Shikake-waza

By Prof. Ōya Minoru (Kendo Kyōshi 7-dan)
International Budo University

Translated by Alex Bennett

(1) Katsugi-waza

Katsugi-waza is used to tempt your opponent (temptation technique). Looking for the right opportunity, the *shinai* is suddenly lifted over the left shoulder. The opponent will think there is an opening and start to lift their hands to strike. As soon as their *kensen* begins to move, seize the moment and strike first.

(2) Maki-waza

Maki-waza entails a circular bind of the opponent's *shinai* from the left or right side, upwards or downwards. This essentially breaks the opponent's *kamae* and creates openings.

(3) Hari-waza (*another term for *harai-waza*)

When the opponent's *kamae* is unyielding, step in and use the *shinogi* (side) of the *monouchi* to slap the opponent's *shinai* directly from the side, around the middle section. Immediately follow up with an attack as a hole appears in their *kamae*. The verb "*haru*" is the same used in the sumo technique "*hari-te*" (open hand strike).

Slapping the *shinai* strongly from the side will unlock the opponent's *kamae*, but this technique should be executed with accompanying footwork to be effective, not just with the hands. In other words, step in while striking the *shinai* with a short sharp motion. Snapping up the left foot together with the slap makes it more effective, and sets you up to launch by bringing the *kensen* back to the centre so you can strike without delay.

The middle of the *tsuka* should serve as the fulcrum when executing *hari-waza*. This means that the snapping motion of both the left and right wrists, *tenouchi*, and the flow on to the strike must be unbroken. If the wrists are used well in *hari*, the *shinai* should automatically return to the centre. The *hari* and ensuing strike should be done in one movement rather than two.

(4) Katate-waza

Katate-waza is a kind of "projectile weapon" useful for surprising your opponent. Done with one hand, it garners more reach than standard two-handed techniques, but

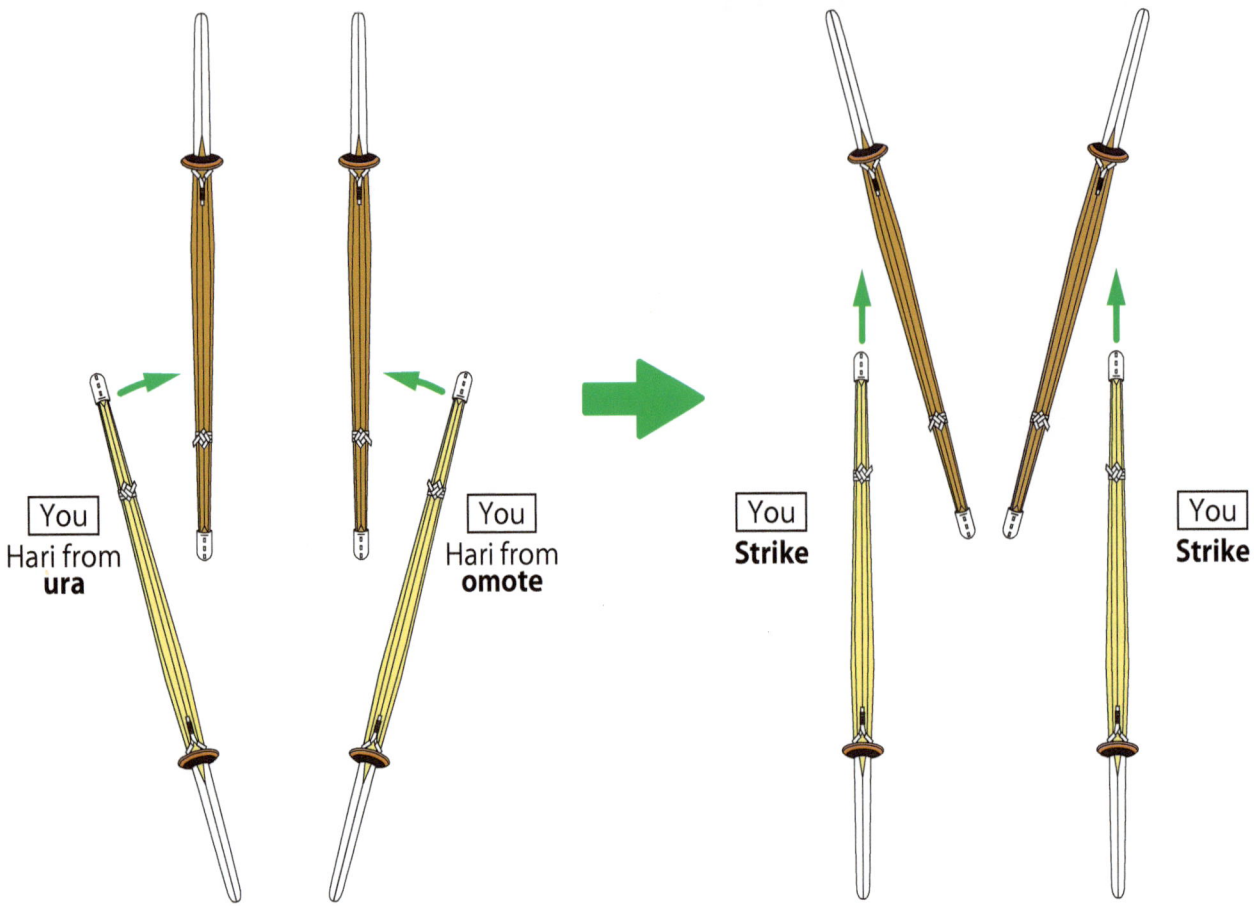

timing and distance is vitally important; it will not work from close in.

(5) General Considerations

I have offered brief introductions of *katsugi-waza*, *maki-waza*, *hari-waza*, and *katate-waza*. In the case of *katsugi-waza*, although the *shinai* is brought back to the left shoulder to generate a hole in your opponent's defence (*kyo*), this also has the effect of leaving you exposed as well. Both *maki-waza* and *hari-waza* are used for destabilising the opponent's posture and *kamae* before striking. When done correctly, they can be very effective in destroying the opponent's *kamae*; but if it is not seamlessly followed up they will have time to react to the ensuing strike.

If you look at the mindset of people doing *maki-waza*, it is often when they are being quite aggressive. Being a powerful movement when executed properly, *maki-waza* can become habitual. If this happens, and *maki-waza* becomes the "go to" technique, this will be to the detriment of one's kendo development. The practitioner will begin to neglect other subtler aspects of their kendo, so care should be taken. Also, as *katate-waza* is a kind of "projectile" used to surprise your opponent, it will become ineffectual if used too much. The same can be said for all of these techniques. They should be applied to probe your opponent in the "toing and froing". Categorised as *shikake-waza*, you will come across them here and there in *keiko* and *shiai*, but they are comparatively uncommon. In any case, you should know the techniques and understand how to use them, but do not become preoccupied with them. Ultimately, rather than "surprise techniques", assailing your opponent front-on, pressuring and willing them to open up, then seizing the hole that manifests in their posture and mind is what all kendoka should be aspiring to.

In my next instalment, I will analyse *ōji-waza*.

"Jippatsu kyū-chū"
"Ten shots, nine hits."

There is no such thing as 100 per cent success, but you at least aim for 99.

Yoshida Ōkura (1588–1644), a famous archer and son of Yoshida Shigekata, a pioneer of early archery traditions.

Yoshida Ōkura Shigeuji was born the third son of Yoshida Shigekata in 1588, towards the end of the turbulent Warring States period. According to the Edo period almanac of all things martial, *Bugei shōden*, "Night and day Ōkura focused on his archery and became greatly skilled." He was even called "an immortal" of archery, and created his own style (Ōkura-ha) based on the Heki-ryū tradition.

His reputation preceded him, and his celebrity status as an archer par excellence was greatly augmented by his incredible feat of dexterity at the Sanjūsangendō Temple in Kyoto. At the celebrated *tōshiya* tournament, he shot 2087 arrows in 24 hours, of which 1330 successfully made it down the long corridor, giving him a new record for total number of arrows and a highly respectable 63.4% success rate. Many tried and failed to emulate the "god of continuous shooting", and his legend lives on to this day.

At one stage in his career, he served Maeda Toshitsune, daimyo of the Kaga domain, and received a generous stipend of 1400-*koku*—enough rice to feed 1400 people in a year. He was clearly a popular addition to Toshitsune's entourage, and his sublime skill in archery was demonstrated over and over. For example, on a falconry excursion, his lord's favourite bird flew off his arm and landed high in the branches of a tall tree. Alas for the falcon, its leash got caught in the branches, and it became well-and-truly stuck. Alas for Shigeuji, Toshitsune ordered him to free the bird with an arrow, but to make sure that his

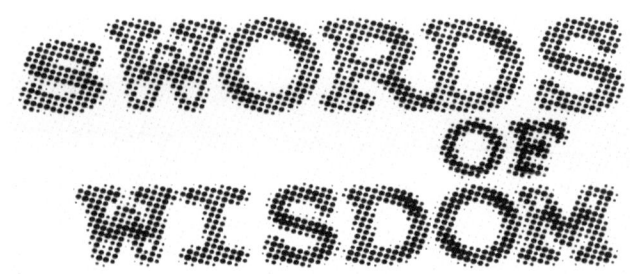

By
ALEX BENNETT
Based on the book
"KENSHI NO MEIGON" (1998)
by the late Tobe Shinjūrō
Used with author's permission.

feathered servant wasn't injured in any way… Shigeuji took careful aim and cut through the leash with the arrow. A truly maginificant shot. The falcon fluttered back down to its master without a scratch, albeit somewhat freaked out by its near-death experience.

Shigeuji once was making his way back from Kyoto and stopped off at an inn in Ōmi. The proprietor was in a terrible state as his child had become bewitched by a fox. The innkeeper pleaded with Shigeuji to rid his house of such evil, even if it meant taking the life of his child. Shigeuji made him sign a pledge not to "sue his butt" should the unfortunate child be killed in the "exorcism by arrow". The kid was tied up, and Shigeuji proceeded to draw his bow. When the fox spirit realised that it was his butt on the line now, it vacated its young host and ran for its life. This story was passed on through the generations as a metaphor for the bow's powerful function as an instrument of morality and purity.

In yet another story highlighting Shigeuji's brilliance, an accomplished archer once paid him a visit and challenged him to a shooting match. The challenger wielded an enormous bow that most mere mortals would never have the strength to pull. The challenge was to shoot an arrow through a Japanese pagoda tree, known for its virtually impenetrable hardwood. The challenger fired first, and his arrow just managed to pass through the trunk. Indeed, this was a formidable show of brute force. Shigeuji then ran back into his house and bizarrely selected a decidedly weak bow. He set up for the shot and released his arrow in a most unimpressive display of power. With little oomph in the bow, the arrow seemed to fly in slow motion toward the tree. Then, miraculously, it passed through the trunk and lodged itself in a stone wall on the other side. The challenger muttered in disbelief as he retreated, bow between his legs. Upon closer inspection, Shigeuji's arrow had evidently passed through the hole made in the trunk by the challenger's arrow. "It's not about brawn" he said, "but how you use your brain."

Skilled, smart, and also very modest was Shigeuji. He was a staunch advocate of the ideal that archery was not about whether the arrow hits the target or not. It was far more profound than that. Becoming one with the arrow and the target was the ultimate objective, and this was not always the case even if the shot was accurate.

A Kaga samurai named Toyoshima Shinshichirō was a renowned marksman. He made a beautiful musket and thought to engrave "*hyaku-patsu hyaku-chū*" (100 shots, 100 hits) on the barrel as a present to his lord. Shigeuji took issue with the inscription and advised Shinshichirō "Perhaps something a little less audacious would be prudent. Something like… 100 shots, 99 hits?" His advice went unheeded. Shigeuji in turn fashioned his lord a bow, and on it he inscribed "*jū no kyū*" (9 out of 10). The lord loved the bow, but the gun not so much.

Behind this oxymoron, perhaps, was the notion that even the one shot that misses the target might well be the most spiritually replete shot of one's life.

Yamamoto Mariko Seminar

By Diana C. Kitthajaroenchai

The Georgia Kendo Association (GKA) was very fortunate to have Yamamoto Mariko-sensei and Sasamori Kanako-sensei visit us for a seminar from January 16 to 17, 2016. It was held at the Lifetime Fitness Center at Johns Creek, Georgia and was attended by over 90 participants from all over the United States, including Puerto Rico. It is always such a great honour to have guests from Japan, but these two amazing ladies were particularly special as we rarely receive female kenshi as guests, let alone such a famous one! We are extremely blessed that Kunitoshi Arai-sensei, the head instructor and president of the GKA, is able to bring such prestigious players to our club. It is definitely our goal to help bring beautiful kendo to share with our fellow kenshi in the Southeast as well as the USA (as our seminars are normally open to anyone).

Yamamoto-sensei's seminar was a truly beautiful experience for us, not only because she is very talented and has won many competitions, but in our opinion, she really embodies the spirit of kendo. Hard work is the key to building a strong foundation, and you cannot expect to be great without mastering the basics.

Unlike many of our other past guests, who are often more experienced and older 8-dan sensei that speak about the spirit of kendo (including her father, Yamamoto Masahiko), or younger talented kenshi who focus on the physical techniques of kendo (like Kiwada Daiki), Yamamoto-sensei really emphasised the importance of core physical and mental training. Instead of focusing on muscle strength through thousands of *suburi*, it was about toning all parts of the body required to make your strikes cleaner and sharper. We did many squat exercises, as well as large stretch hits to work our backs and shoulder blades. She also showed us some finesse exercises where we would rotate our *shinai* in circles around our partner's so that we could develop the proper wrist and forearm muscles needed for flexible strikes.

Yamamoto-sensei also focused on the correct *kamae* position for hands, and gave the following pointers:

1. Always hold the left hand at the absolute bottom of the *shinai*
2. Keep the grip in a diamond shape, similar to holding a gun, with the strength of the grip only in the small, ring, and middle fingers

3. Hold the *shinai* lightly and at the correct distance from the body during practice and matches so that you can make a full extension for proper snap

Yamamoto-sensei often commented that on the whole, we were using too much strength, which made our strikes painful to receive. The more we were able to relax, the better our *tenouchi* would be. She also showed us a couple of exercises that many Japanese high school and professional kendo players do: put your hands together and rotate your thumbs in clockwise and counter-clockwise directions to train the brain for flexibility and small muscle movements.

Yamamoto-sensei also spoke about developing good habits for *suriashi* foot movements. She explained this in two sections: *suriashi* and *fumikomi*. These are very important towards achieving a good strike. Starting with the *tanden* (which many teachers have mentioned), the body must always use the core muscles to push forward. But to accompany this, she explained that the left foot must follow swiftly, almost in a hopping motion that would complete the strike. Both Yamamoto-sensei and Sasamori-sensei had excellent footwork in this regard. They have different styles, but both were able to achieve multiple hits in succession or from any *maai* because of their core body work and swift left leg movements.

The second section was in regards to *fumikomi*, or the stomp that accompanies a *men* strike. Yamamoto-sensei showed us that she imagines the right foot makes a gripping motion, similar to what an octopus does with its suction cups. Rather than lifting the foot up and down to stomp, she moves forward and tries to grip the ground with her entire foot and toes.

These elements of core muscles, a swift left foot, and proper right foot grip really showed excellent footwork from both ladies. Good footwork allows you to complete a strike and make the body ready for the next.

Even though Yamamoto-sensei is small, her strikes were extremely sharp and quick, but never painful. Her footwork was light and had real purpose, while her *fumikomi* was extremely loud. After her demonstrations, she would break down each section and ask us to try them. She also commented that even she did not move on to the next *waza* until she had mastered the first. She commented that she had been working on her *kote* strike for many years, perfecting it, before she could allow herself to move on to the next.

During the question and answer session, Yamamoto-sensei was asked how she mentally prepares for a tournament beforehand and how she feels during them. She told us that she only imagines herself winning first place, and her family and friends congratulating her. During her matches, she said her mind is clear of thoughts but filled with music so she can just depend on her body and reflexes to do as they would do best due to her hard training.

One of the best parts about having a female sensei is being able to see that technique can overcome the odds. It was exciting watching her fight all of the men, and taking many *ippon*! The techniques she shared with us resonated with myself and many others, and we are now working hard in every practice to try and follow her advice regarding footwork, *kamae*, and perseverance.

Yamamoto-sensei was also extremely humble and very patient with us, and I felt that both her and her guest, Sasamori-sensei, really enjoyed sharing their experiences of kendo with us, and really motivated us to push ourselves and make them proud.

J-Concepts' Samurai Green Tea

Samurai Green Tea

Traditional Green Tea from Makinohara City, Shizuoka Prefecture, Japan

ADVERTISEMENT

The Samurai Green Tea Fundraising System

No matter how much we love kendo, the costs involved in it can at times put a strain on even the deepest of wallets. Buying a quality set of *bōgu* can require a big financial commitment, and we've all spent good money on a *shinai* only for it to break after a few training sessions. An even greater expense are the costs involved in travelling to major competitions.

With the exception of kendoka from the major kendo countries such as Japan, Korea and the U.S., many competitors receive little or no financial support from their federation and will have to largely pay their own way to compete in major competitions like the WKC. In order to help meet the costs of travel, some competitors or federations will undertake activities like sponsored *suburi-athons*. It is also difficult for small clubs and federations to purchase the equipment necessary to carry out their activities. With these issues in mind, J-Concepts and Kendo World have collaborated to bring you the Samurai Green Tea Fundraising System to help you raise money for your club, federation or competition travel expenses.

So what exactly is the Samurai Green Tea Fundraising System and how can it help you?

First, Samurai Green Tea comes from Makinohara City in Shizuoka prefecture. This is the heart of Japan's "tea country", and is an area synonymous with the finest green tea. Strongly linked to kendo, this tea actually comes from plantations founded by samurai-come-tea grower, Chūjō Kageaki, whose fascinating story is in the following pages. One canister of Samurai Green Tea contains 20 freshly-packed teabags that can be used to make hot or cold tea. You would order a

Seito Kenyukai Original Label

minimum of one pack of 24 canisters of Samurai Green Tea for $312, which includes postage to anywhere in the world. This works out to be $13 per canister. Next, sell them at the RRP of $19.95, and the profit you make can then go towards paying for travelling expenses, new club *bōgu*, or whatever it is that you need to raise money for.

A unique feature of this product is that you are able to personalise it. Create your own label from scratch or use one of our templates. Once you have placed an order and submitted the label artwork, the tea will be picked and packed, and then labels will be affixed to the canisters. You will receive your totally original canisters of Samurai Green Tea 10–20 days later.

---

1. Contact Graham, your tea and fundraising consultant, at tea@kendo-world.com to see how Samurai Green Tea can help you realise your goal.

2. Design your own label to the required size.

2. Choose one of the many templates and decide what text or photos to use.

3. Submit the label data with your order* and make payment.
   * A minimum order is one carton (24 canisters of 20 tea-bags for $312 including postage to anywhere in the world).

4. Once payment is received, labels will be printed and affixed to canisters.

5. Your tea will then be freshly packed, off the tree not the shelf.

6. Once your product is ready it will be dispatched by international courier.

7. Your carton of customised canisters of tea will arrive 10 to 20 days after confirmation of order depending on your zone. (Delivery times to South America and Africa will take slightly longer.)

8. Sell at the RRP of $19.95 to make $166.80 per carton towards your goal!

9. Still need to raise more funds?

10. No. Buy more tea because it tastes great!

10. Yes. Then buy more tea!

Of course, Samurai Green Tea need not only be bought for fundraising. It can also be used as a commemorative gift to give to friends or family.

Members of Canterbury Kendo Club that were selected to represent New Zealand at the 16th WKC in Tokyo used the Samurai Green Tea Fundraising System to help finance their trip to Japan. Here's what they had to say about it:

"The Samurai Green Tea was a low cost and hugely beneficial aspect of our fund raising efforts to get to the 16th WKC. The option to customise the label made it simple to sell to club members, family and friends. Additionally, as it is green tea, people needed little convincing of its practical value in comparison to other fund raising items we were selling."—Blake Bennett

"Fundraising has always been a tricky one for the Kendo Club. Over the years and campaigns, inevitably the same friends and family get asked for money or labour at various sausage sizzles and suburi-athons etc. This time, it was really nice to be able to offer them something back for their support. Even better, something relevant to kendo with the custom label and link to Japanese culture, and really good tea, too. A great fundraising tool that we will certainly be using again."—David Wong

So, why not ease the financial burden on your club or federation and partake in the samurai legacy at the same time? If you are cold, Samurai Green Tea will warm you. If you are too hot, it will cool you. If you are depressed, it will cheer you. If you are excited, it will calm you. Each cup of Samurai Green Tea represents an imaginary voyage. It is liquid wisdom with all of the health benefits Japanese green tea is famous for. Samurai Green Tea is the real deal.

Samurai Green Tea is

- **100% PRODUCED IN JAPAN**
- **100% FREE OF PRESERVATIVES OR ADDITIVES**
- **100% ORIGINAL**
- **100% READY FOR DOJO FUNDRAISING**
- **100% PERSONALISED TO USE AS A QUALITY GIFT FOR ANY OCCASION**
- **100% DELICIOUS AND HEALTHY**

Contact Graham, your tea and fundraising consultant, at tea@kendo-world.com to see how he can help you raise money for your federation or club.

contact us **tea@kendo-world.com**   about **http://www.j-conceptsjapan.com/samurai-tea/**

J-Concepts 1082-1 Ieyama Kawane-cho, Shimada-shi, Shizuoka, 428-0104 JAPAN Tel.: +81 (0)80-3689-5978

鎧兜
A GUIDE TO JAPANESE ARMOUR

By Teruo Orikasa
Photos by Jo Anseeuw

Kaga-zōgan-abumi —Stirrups with Inlay from Kaga Fief

During the Edo period (1603–1878), *zōgan-abumi* (stirrups with inlay)—also known as *Kaga-zōgan-abumi* or *Kaga-gake*—were *meibutsu* (a famous product associated with a particular region) of the Kaga fief. Some of my predecessors have even said that without knowing about their beauty and aesthetics, Japanese crafts cannot be properly addressed. Although there are truly excellent *zōgan-abumi* extant, studies on them are extremely scarce. To illustrate this, Motoya Fumio stated in his study *Kaga-zōgan-abumi* (NKBKHK 87, 1989) that from the 158 stirrups he had examined there was not a single one which he could date with certainty.

When I started to study and collect *Kaga-zōgan-abumi*, two coincidences occurred. The first one concerned *abumi* I bought about twenty years ago at an antique fair in Tokyo. They are signed "Kashū-jū Murasawa Toshinao saku" (加州住村沢代尚作) and I was fascinated by the quality of the workmanship and

- **Name of Piece:**
  kanzesui ni hatō kingin-zōgan abumi
  (Stirrups with a kinzōgan and ginzōgan ornamentation of waves in kanzesui interpretation)
- **Craftsman:**
  Kashū-jū Ichibei Ujimasa saku
  (加州住市兵衛氏政作)

their design. I dated them intuitively to the late Edo period and thought that with some research I would be able to find out something about the craftsman and his affiliation. So I consulted the standard work on the Japanese harness, namely volume four of the *Nihon-bagu-daikan* (Nihon Chūō Keibakai, 1992), and it actually depicts *abumi* signed "Kashū-jū Toshinao saku" (加州住代尚作). Hiroi Yūichi, the author responsible for that section, writes at the same time that not much is known about Toshinao,

so my studies suffered a rather abrupt setback. In 1998 I discovered a document called *Senzo-yuisho narabi-ichirui zukechō* which contains information on the *zōgan* craftsmen employed by the Kaga fief. This was the second coincidence as I learned therein of the genealogy and scholastic background of Toshinao, and that his full name was actually Murasawa Hanzaemon Toshinao.

Since then, I have been captivated by *Kaga-zōgan-abumi* and have focused my research on *zōgan-abumi* by the craftsmen working for the Kaga fief. For several years now I have tried to shed some light on this topic, and as such, I would like to introduce a set of *abumi* here.

The roundish upper part of the *emi* speaks for *Kyō-gake*, i.e. Kyoto-style stirrups. The inlay is in *kinzōgan* and *ginzōgan,* and the so-called *kanzesui* wave interpretation goes over the *kako-gashira*, *kakokubi*, *emi*, *yanaiba* and *ichimonji*. The *shitaura* also features *kinzōgan* and *ginzōgan* ornamentation, namely in the form of a willow. The *sukashi* openings along the *kakokubi* are of the *jūichidan-sangi* (eleven-rung ladder) interpretation and the outside bears laterally the *ginzōgan-mei* "Kashū-jū Ichibei Ujimasa saku".

The *Senzo-yuisho narabi-ichirui zukechō* lists Ichibei Ujimasa as the 4th-generation, and Ichibei Ujimasa as the 5th-generation of the Katsugi Kikumasa family. Both worked as manufacturers of presentation stirrups and bore the rank of *tōdori* (director [of the workshop]). The 4th-generation head died in 1695 and the 5th-generation in 1720. The fact that both were appointed to the rank of *tōdori* speaks for their skill. This lets us assume that they were the leading craftsmen in their field at that time. However, I cannot tell which generation made this pair of stirrups (although I tend to think that we are facing a work of the 4th-generation Ichibei Ujimasa).

References

- Orikasa Teruo, *Kaga-zōgan-kata o-saiku-sha no keifu 6—Katsugi Kikumasa (Kodō) no 'Senzo-yuisho narabi-ichirui zukechō' o chūshin toshite*. NKBKHK combined issues 131 + 132, January 2001
- This article is adapted from a section of the book *Kaga-zōgan-abumi—The Collection of Teruo Orikasa* (2015).
- For more info about Japanese Armour, see www.katchu-no-bi.com

鎧 兜　A GUIDE TO JAPANESE ARMOUR

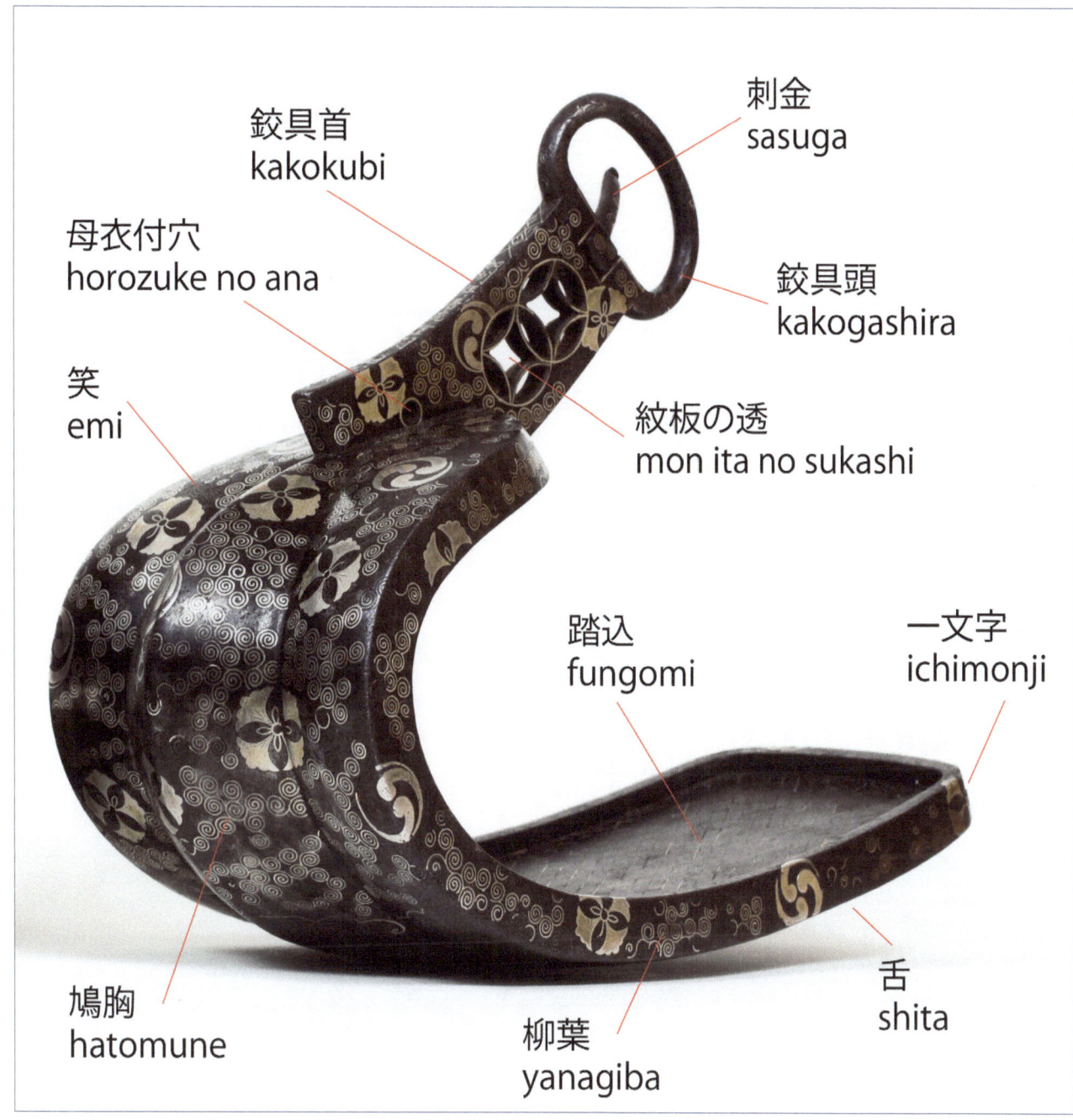

50　*A Guide to Japanese Armour*

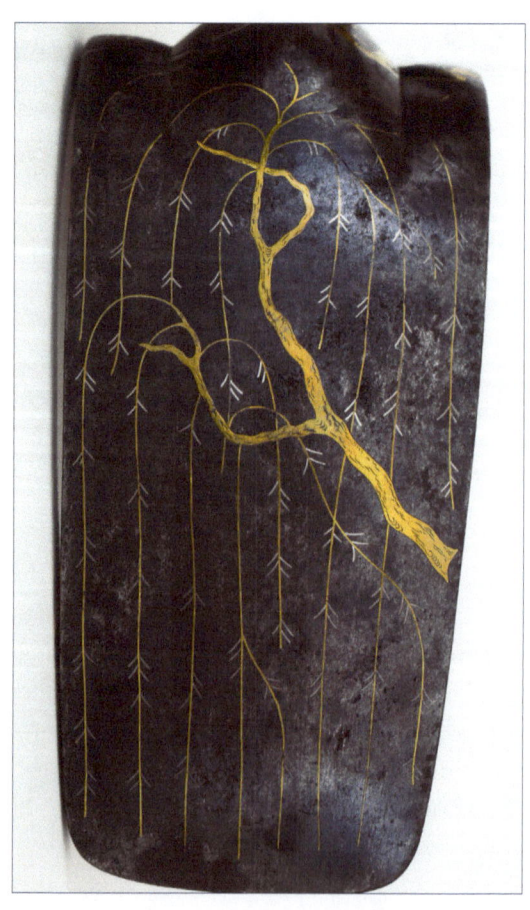

The 2016 Shūdōkai Grading Gasshuku

Report and Translation by Michael Ishimatsu-Prime

November is a big month in the kendo calendar with the All Japan Kendo Championships held on the third day. November is also grading season in Japan with the 8-dan test in Tokyo, and the 6- and 7-dan examinations at several locations around the country. In the run-up to these gradings, the Shūdōkai kendo club holds its annual grading *gasshuku*.

The Shūdōkai kendo club was founded in 1986, and is based in the Inage area of Chiba city. The current Shihan is K8-dan Shigematsu Kimiaki-sensei, a kendo instructor with the Chiba Police Department. The 2016 *gasshuku* was held on October 28 & 29 in the seaside resort town of Kujukuri. A total of 40 Shūdōkai members and guests participated in the event.

Instructors

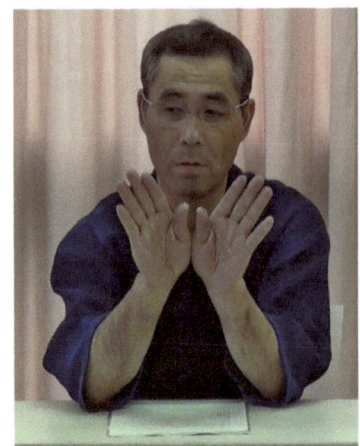

K8-dan Shigematsu Kimiaki

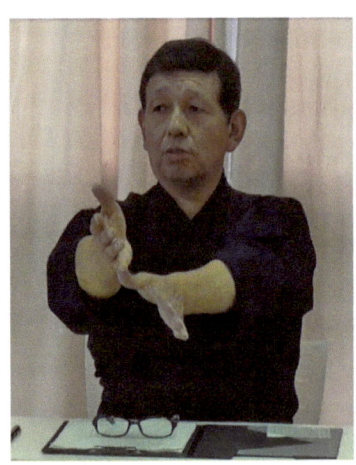

K8-dan Mutō Kazuhiro

The first item on the agenda on Saturday afternoon was a lecture about grading by K8-dan Mutō Kazuhiro-sensei of Keishichō (Tokyo Metropolitan Police), followed by another by Shigematsu-sensei. Once the lectures had finished, *gasshuku* participants sat mock gradings from 5- to 8-dan. These were assessed by Shigematsu-sensei and Mutō-sensei, and the examinees were given immediate feedback. Both Mutō-sensei and Shigematsu-sensei regularly serve as examiners at gradings, so their insight is invaluable. This writer would rather forget his mock test, but the resulting feedback proved to be very useful and provided considerable food for thought.

The mock gradings were followed by a keiko session for all participants that ranged in age from their teens to their 80s. This was followed by a bath and the obligatory trip to the second dojo until the early hours to make sure that everyone was in fine fettle for *asa-geiko* at 6:00am on Sunday morning.

What follows are the transcripts of the lectures that were given by Mutō-sensei and Shigematsu-sensei. It will be useful information for those preparing for examinations, and great advice for kendo in general.

Mutō-sensei Lecture

Today, I would like to talk to you about aspects of kendo related to promotion examinations. First, I'd like to ask you this. Is your purpose in kendo to take gradings? It's only one of kendo's goals, but the ideal is "*shōgai* kendo", or kendo for life. I've seen people who were strong when they were elementary or junior high school students, but we often don't hear their names beyond that because they probably lacked a good grounding in *kihon* and were instructed just to score points. This is the fault of their instructors. If they were instructed correctly and learned correct *kihon* from a young age, they would be able to do kendo into their 70s and 80s.

Let's go over some things that are needed to prepare for a grading:

Chakusō

It is important that your equipment—*kendō-gi*, *hakama*, *bōgu*—fits your body correctly. Don't let your *gi* puff out at the back of your *hakama*. It should be pulled down tight. Also, clean the white salt marks from your *gi* that sometimes appear so that it looks presentable and doesn't smell.

The five pleats on the front of the *hakama* and the one at the back must be sharp and straight. The way that the *hakama* is worn is very important. Some people wear their *hakama* hanging low at the back, but the front should be lower. This is very noticeable to the grading panel.

The length of the *men-himo* is set at 40cm from the knot, but it does not have to be exactly that length. Longer might be okay for taller people, but if it looks excessively long, that could be a black mark against you.

How you put on *bōgu* is also important. We all know that the correct way is to put it on while sitting. Paying attention to such things in the course of your daily training means it will become a part of you, which is in turn reflected in your kendo.

Shinai

Use a *shinai* that is suitable for your body type. A female practitioner I know was told by another sensei that to get stronger, she should use a heavier *shinai*. I think this advice is wrong: she should go lighter. Use a *shinai* that is suitable for your body.

When striking, we use the shoulder joints, then the elbows, and then the wrists. When you use a heavier *shinai*, the joints used the most will be the shoulders; but with a lighter *shinai* it's the elbows and wrists. We know that the wrists are maybe the most important part of the strike to get the final snap, so the lighter the *shinai* the more the wrists are used.

For the lady that I mentioned, if she used a heavier *shinai* it would mean her hits would be solid for sure; but in reality, she did not have the physical strength to wield it effectively. I therefore recommended that she use a lighter *shinai*.

Men should also find the ideal *shinai* weight for their body, and then use a slightly lighter one. They will be able to strike more effectively with their wrists. Of course, shoulders and elbows should still be used, but percentage-wise, the wrists should constitute about 50 per cent of the strike; elbows, 30; and shoulders, 20. Try thinking about these percentages in *keiko*. Experiment using the shoulders most, elbows most, and wrists most. You should find that the wrists are the fastest. Executing a big *kihon* strike will require use of the shoulders, but it will be slow. It is easier to strike with *ki-ken-tai-itchi*—something necessary in a grading—when using a lighter *shinai*.

Nakayui

The purpose of the *nakayui* is to keep the *shinai* together, and prevent it from injuring your opponent. The ideal positioning is a quarter of the *shinai*'s length from the *kensen*. In reality, however, the *nakayui* is often not placed here; it is often around a fifth of the length from the tip. Be careful with this. In a *shinsa*, the position of the *nakuyui* is easily seen by the examiners. It is not something that people will tell you about, but you should pay attention to it.

Tsuba

Make sure that there is no gap between the *tsuba* and the *habaki* (collar of the *tsukagawa*). This is often seen at the elementary school level, but it's not acceptable in a grading.

Hassei

This is a crucial part of a grading. When the examination begins and you stand up, don't rush to *kiai*: let your opponent *kiai* first, and then try to smother it with your own *kiai*. Letting your opponent *kiai* first might not seem like a good idea, but this has appeal for the examiners. It is like you are trying to control your opponent with your *kiai*. This is something that everyone should be able to do, but in a grading examinees are usually nervous, and *kiai* as soon as they stand up. If your opponent does not *kiai* when you stand up from *sonkyo*, however, don't just stand there and wait for them. There is limited time in a grading time so you need to take that into consideration. I *kiai* in this way at gradings, and in *keiko* and *shiai*. I have made it my own style. My *kiai* pattern might suit you, or it might not. But it's worth trying. If it doesn't suit you, drop it and think of your own way.

Kamae

Kendo starts and ends with *kamae*. *Kakari-geiko* and *kirikaeshi* are a tough part of kendo training, but doing it a lot it gives you power in your *tanden* (lower abdominal region) and cultivates a strong *kamae*. Examiners can tell if you have this power by observing your *kamae*. It's not only *kakari-geiko* or *kirikaeshi*, however, but all tough experiences in your life that help you nurture this power, or presence, in your *kamae*. You shouldn't think of work and kendo as being separate things. In this sense, even if you haven't done lots of *kakari-geiko* and *kirikaeshi* in your youth, it doesn't mean that you can't have a strong *kamae*. Use the other experiences from your life to help bolster your kendo.

Kihon

Kihon and basic body movement are something that you always need to revisit. For example, keeping the feet straight. If your left foot turns slightly, you will need to twist it to move forward. The Achilles is strong when straight, but weak when twisted.

The wrists, too, are also very important. Some think that when people make powerful strikes it is because they are physically strong. This is not the reason. It is because they are using their body efficiently, and making the wrists snap. They have good balance between the left and right arms. Importantly, they only use the muscles that are needed while the other parts are relaxed. There is no unnecessary power. Striking in this manner will result in strong strikes, and enable you to do kendo for a long time.

If you continue to do "uneven" kendo, it will eventually become your style. I see some people's *suburi* is excellent, but when they start *keiko*, that form disappears. They are only thinking about hitting their opponent; not keeping their form. Straight kendo will eventually make you strong. If you are doing wonky kendo when you are young, maybe you can strike a successful *ippon*, but if you carry on like this you will eventually be unable to strike successfully and need to resort to using tricks to win.

Straight kendo trumps all, eventually. This is what old sensei often say, but it is difficult. When I was a competitor in the police, I needed to win and I couldn't think about doing straight kendo. I now understand how important it is. *Suburi* helps this a lot.

When doing *kirikaeshi*, put all your effort into making the last *men* strike as solid as possible. Don't make that last strike at an angle. The manner of your last *men* strike will dictate improvement in your kendo.

Shigematsu-sensei Lecture

When you seek advice from the sensei that you practised with during *keiko*, you might be told the same thing over and over. With that in mind, what I'm going to talk to you about from now may be old hat, and may double over with what Mutō-sensei covered, but that means it's important.

A grading is a place where you can demonstrate your kendo. The kendo that you show in a grading should be your normal kendo, not a type of kendo only for gradings. Practice makes perfect only if practising things perfectly. Attention to detail is vital.

Chakusō

Like Mutō-sensei mentioned earlier, *chakusō* is an important part of a grading, especially the way the *men* is worn. He mentioned *men-himo*, but another thing to keep in mind is whether or not the examinee is looking through the *monomi* of the *mengane*. The examiners are sitting side-on to the examinees, and it looks very strange if the *monomi* is too high or low. Please make sure that it is directly in front of the eyes.

Another aspect of *chakusō* is the collar and lapels of the *gi*. They should be neat and straight, and close fitting to the body.

Stand up straight when you put the *hakama* on. If you lean your body forward as you tie the *himo*, the back will end up being lower that the front when you then stand up straight.

Reihō

Reihō (protocols of etiquette) is another important part of a grading. As prescribed by the AJKF, the correct way in which to perform *rei* is with the heels touching and the feet pointing out at an angle. If the heels are not touching, this is not correct *rei*, and will be marked down.

Sonkyo

Some people lean forward when they stand up from *sonkyo*. When crouching in *sonkyo*, you should have a straight back, and stand as if being pulled up by the hair on your head. Similarly, go down into *sonkyo* as if being pulled down by the hair. You need good strength in your knees and legs.

Shinai Grip

When gripping the *shinai*, the end of the *tsukagawa* should not be visible from the left hand. This is easy to see for the examiners, and again, gives the examinee a "minus image". Some people keep opening and closing the left grip, but you should maintain a firm grip with the left hand, and the little finger should be closed completely.

Kihaku (Spirit)

I passed the 8-dan grading in 2009, but before that I attended a seminar at which Chiba-sensei gave the following advice: "If your opponent's *kihaku* is at the level of 100, yours should be at 150. If your opponent's is at 150, yours should be at 200." Tahara-sensei also said, "A grading is not about *datotsu*. It's about what happens until the strike is made, or until the *waza* is executed."

Waza

Study *waza* in which you take the initiative. It is easy to impress the examiners if you can do *debana-men* or *debana-gote*. That is, make your opponent execute a *waza* but then strike with your own. Do not just wait for your opponent to strike. There's a big difference between your opponent being *able* to strike, and being *made* to strike.

Shokujin and Kōha

Shokujin and *kōha* are the distances at which two kendoka face each other; *shokujin* being where the *shinai* are not crossed, and *kōha* where they do. These terms are not used by the AJKF, which uses *tōma*, *issoku ittō-no-maai*, and *chikama*.

In a fight with a *katana*, the encounter starts with the *kissaki* slightly touching. Moving in quickly without thinking is something that elementary, middle, and high school students usually do, and far removed from the ideal of using a *katana*.

Some sensei say that waiting at the *shokujin* distance is the most mentally calm interval, and allows you to execute *waza* quickly and resolutely. From this position, you can strike or be struck by taking one step (*issoku-ittō-no-maai*). This is the distance at which a person's mental power is forged.

In the move from *shokujin* to *kōha*, three things can happen: 1) you move in from *shokujin* to *kōha*; 2) your opponent moves into *kōha*; 3) both enter the fighting interval of *kōha*. I think that it is important to take the initiative yourself and close the *maai*. However, when moving into the *kōha* position, this is the distance at which you are likely to stiffen up and suffer from one of the "*shikai*", or four sicknesses.

It is okay to be struck. The worst thing you can do is move the head to the side, or back, to avoid your opponent's strike. This shows one of the "four sicknesses" (fear, surprise, doubt, hesitation). Perhaps the biggest "sickness" is "*uchitai, uchitai*" (I want to strike, I want to strike), and this is the most common problem in a grading. Another sickness occurs when you have moved forward and closed the *maai*.

At this close distance, many people cannot keep the pressure up, and they move their left foot backward slightly. At an AJKF *keiko* that I attended in the summer, I saw Iwasa Hidenori, a former All Japan Champion who recently passed the 8-dan grading on his third attempt, face H8-dan Iwatate Saburō-sensei. Iwasa is a very strong competitor, but as Iwatate-sensei pressured Iwasa, his left foot moved back. If you move your left foot back, you cannot attack or execute *kaeshi-waza*. If you cannot do that in regular *keiko*, you will not be able to in a match.

In the National Sports Meet (Kokutai) in Wakayama in 2015, I was the Taishō of the Chiba team, and we faced Iwate prefecture in the quarterfinal match. When it came to the Taishō round, the match was tied and I needed to win to ensure that we progressed. I moved into the *kōha* position to pressure my opponent, but thought that as the match could be decided in *enchō*, I did not need to hurry to get the *ippon*. So, I backed away. This was careless on my part, and after that I just could not get back into the match. My *seme* was incomplete, and before the end of regulation time, I conceded a *tsuki*. We lost, and our tournament was over. In matches and gradings, it is very important not to move your left foot back, so please think about this.

Right, time for *keiko*.

Guidelines to Kendo Promotional Examinations
Part 1   By Jeff Marsten (Kendo Kyōshi 7-dan)

Gradings linger in the shadow of shiai
If this is so, then all future hope is lost
Winning is here today and gone tomorrow
Yet development has no end.
— Tanka Poem

International Kendo Federation: "The Concept of Kendo":

Kendo is a way to discipline the human character through the application of the principles of the Katana.

This article is a compilation of the thinking and experience of many sensei over kendo's long development to the place we are today. The content has been collated from oral tradition and written material, and is pertinent to understanding the grading system and its underlying philosophy in modern kendo. The following questions are often raised: Why is there a grading system in kendo? Is it fair? Does it make any sense?

We often encounter people with the same grade, yet their skill level is obviously not the same. Note also that individuals under the rank of *shodan* may be

the "head sensei" of a club or dojo geographically removed from mainstream kendo areas. This is unheard of in Japan, but is why the lower *dan* grades take on more weight outside Japan than in. It is hoped that this article will allow for a better understanding of the purpose, criteria, and method of taking promotional examinations.

First, the grading system brings order where there would be chaos in the same way that rules bring lawfulness to *shiai*. Without a grading system, the structure of the dojo would deteriorate into "who is the best stick hitter", and not take into account deeper knowledge and leadership skills. Ranks provide kendo aficionados an achievable goal for progress. The ability to do beautiful kendo is not necessarily dictated by scoring points, but it is wonderful when the two come together.

Great athletes are not always good teachers, and do not necessarily have an ability to transfer their knowledge of what to do, and how to do it. The best of both worlds is when an individual can both perform *and* teach. The grading system provides a method to enhance one's kendo by providing structure, and recognition of improvement. Teachers should support students' goals to advance up the ranks, and provide opportunities to polish skills and knowledge to this end.

Starting in the late 1990s, the All Japan Kendo Federation (AJKF) re-evaluated how individuals should be judged in promotion examinations. In 2006, the International Kendo Federation (FIK) moved to further set criteria to define each rank. Because the lower *kyū* grades are for children, and are awarded at the dojo or local federation level, no criteria have been established by the international body. This has left non-Japanese kendo organisations to work out criteria as they see fit. The result is a hodgepodge of what constitutes a *kyū* grade. Generally speaking, adult students have difficulty balancing work and family obligations and getting in the hours of required kendo practice. Moreover, in most countries outside Japan, there are few children doing kendo. This reality skews the perception and standards of what each *kyū* grade represents.

When there were 10-dan masters in Japan, they were thought of as representing 100% and *shodan* 10% of the ideal. As there are no longer any 10-dan in Japan and the highest rank that can now be awarded is 8-dan, this resulted in necessary adjustments to the requirements for each *dan*. Recently, many AJKF leaders have been lamenting that the bar was possibly set too high. The reality in other federations throughout the world is never going to be the same as in Japan.

As per the official "Concept of Kendo" promulgated in 1975 by the AJKF, personal development is the stated purpose or goal of kendo, rather than obtaining grades or winning tournaments. Promotion examinations only provide measurement to some aspects of the stated purpose of kendo. Personal development, however, has many more components than those gauged by ranking system criteria. *Dan* ranks can be thought of as mileposts along the path (*dō/michi*) of kendo. Sensei, or those who have gone before, look back down the path and recognise students who have reached a destination for *kyū* or *dan* based on their own experiences. In this sense, each examination board is a composite of individuals and their collective experiences. They measure your kendo against their understanding of the standard set forth by the FIK.

Getting past their personal core beliefs and accepting a stipulated standard is difficult to say the least. The outcome is that the makeup of any given examination board will determine the results of an examination. As such, each federation conducting grading examinations has a responsibility to ensure that its examiners are thoroughly trained, and that the results are transparent. Too often an unsuccessful candidate will go to the examiners afterwards and receive five or six different answers as to why they failed. Individuals who pass, on the other hand, will walk away satisfied and not question the process.

So, what responsibility does the examining organisation have with regard to individuals being graded? If people are satisfied, then the event is said to have been a success. There will be no need or desire for

feedback, and hence no accountability on the part of the examination board. Clearly this is not an acceptable scenario. Each federation has a duty to ensure transparency, accountability, clear standards, and preparation to offer apposite feedback irrespective of the results with each grading.

What steps can be taken to facilitate this? First, it is helpful to take a page out of the *shiai* process. Plenty of effort is put into holding *shinpan* seminars, *shiai* practice, and special coaching sessions. There is a rule book defining and explaining what a valid strike consists of, and how matches should be adjudicated. There is a clear link between *shinsa* and *shiai*, in that the criteria for valid strikes is the same, and those who referee matches will also apply the same objective views when assessing the merits of a candidate in a grading. However, there are also some fundamental differences in what is expected in a grading compared to a competition. Understanding the differences is key to being a superior *shinpan* and *shinsa-in*.

To pass the 8-dan test you must strike a clear, decisive blow that demonstrates total commitment of body and mind to the attack. In order to accomplish this you must first cut the opponent mentally. This concept is the same for all grades actually, but becomes increasingly refined in *shinsa* for the upper *dan* grades (6-8). If perfect strikes were necessary in competition, however, then most matches would end in a draw, or have to be decided by referees' decision (*hantei*). A *shinpan* and *shinsa-in* must be able to resolve this issue with the ability to make adjustments depending on the required skill level of competitors in different divisions. The bar for what constitutes a valid strike is not the same in the junior, adult beginner, and advanced divisions of a tournament. Similarly, if you are sitting on a grading panel, you must be able to differentiate the requirements of each *kyū* or *dan* being graded. This makes for an interesting quandary regarding the *kyū* grades as the only *kyū* defined by the FIK is *ikkyū*. *Kyū* grades vary greatly between various international kendo bodies, and even within member countries that have multiple sub-organisations.

Historically, *kyū* grades were established to help children progress, and usually awarded at the club or dojo level. This provides the child with recognition of progress, level of effort, and a goal to be obtained. With the dissemination of kendo outside of Japan, several things happened. First, adults became beginners and each organisation defined its standards. One of the benefits of the FIK was the issuance of a standard definition of the requirements for *ikkyū*

through to 8-dan. These are not finite, and are quite general in their description of the requirements for each level.

The *menjo* and rank you receive after passing *shinsa* is recognition by those that have gone before you of your attainment of proficiency at that level. It is up to each organisation to standardise and communicate what the process consists of. Standardisation and communication would ideally come through a training process to set levels and gain consensus among individuals in the examiner pool, and also educate and prepare new examiners.

Your own ability to pass *shinsa* does not equate to being a qualified *shinpan* or *shinsa-in*. Judging candidates in an examination requires training, just as the referees are encouraged to undergo. In both cases, there are those who will never fully acquire enough skill. This is precisely why *shinpan* and *shinsa-in* require some method to establish measurability, reliability, and validity. When these conditions do not exist, the entire process is called into question. Just as the awarding of *ippon* needs to be understood by the audience, competitors, and *shinpan* in *shiai*, the *shinsa* process must also be comprehended by all stakeholders. When test results are tainted by what is perceived as favouritism, a lack of clarity or reasonableness, the system will be viewed as suspect, and rightly so.

Measures for consistency need to be applied, and examiners falling outside the normal standards have to be addressed. This means examiners who administer a pass rate that is either too high or too low, should be informed of their differing criteria and helped to adjust. Or, they should be removed from the pool of examiners.

A standardised grading sheet with check boxes for required skills that are missing in the candidate will go a long way towards levelling out the process. Additionally, a candidate should never get five or six different reasons about why they failed, and what needs to be fixed. If they are presented with so many conflicting pieces of information, it means the examiners are unreliable. No one will be able to have confidence in the results, even those who pass. If this describes your organisation's examination process, then the leadership must take corrective action to remedy the situation.

Federations are not dojo. They exist to conduct and provide activities a dojo cannot. These activities include large scale tournaments, promotion examinations, and overall education. If the organisation does not provide these services, then it has no need

to exist. Kendo organisations in the various member countries of the FIK not only operate in accordance to the cultural norms of that country, but also by the makeup of the membership. The exportation of kendo from Japan is a conundrum. Japanese leadership has truly endeavoured to support the international dissemination of kendo, but messages usually get jumbled down the chain of command. Gradings are a good example of this, and is why the same amount of effort put into training *shinpan* should also be afforded to nurturing examiners.

The following is a list of steps that can be taken to improve examinations:

- A clear understanding by the examiners of the requirements and criteria of each rank.
- Further development and discussion of the FIK 2006 Criteria.
- Regular training seminars for *shinsa-in*.
- Practice exams where each examiner's results are reviewed. This will help to develop a common understanding and consensus among examiners.
- A standard grading sheet that allows examiners to provide feedback by means of a check list.
- Pre-exam debriefing seminars to reflect on the results.

To take the example of the AUSKF and its member federations, criteria as to what constitutes a given rank are becoming more uniform. It seems to me that a couple of sub-federations still have their respective bars set a little low. As the number of 7-dan sensei outside California increases, and more interaction is happening among the AUSKF kendo population, standards are becoming much closer overall.

An area that should be of concern to the AUSKF is the extremely poor pass rate for those taking the 5-dan examination. The current pass rate hovers around 10%, while in Japan it is about 20%. The historical rate for 6-dan is about 13%-15%, and 10% for 7-dan. The AUSKF cannot be compared on the 6- and 7-dan pass rates because the sample pool is just too small. The 5-dan pool in the US is similar to the smaller AJKF regional federations.

I would suggest the following: 1. That 4-dan are prepared to become examiners for the juniors, and 5-dan educated to assess adult *kyū* tests; 2. Clearer standards are set for *shodan* to 3-dan as a lead on to 4-dan. To improve the quality of examination boards, a system of selection of examiners and training needs to be implemented to ensure the criteria for each level is being abided by.

When businesses hold quality improvement circles, much of the work done upfront is on developing the problem statement. A Quality Circle is formed to analyse and resolve problems in manufacturing a product. In kendo's case, the product is providing the students with valid assessment procedures for measuring of certain aspects of their kendo. The criteria for each *dan* grade are outlined in very broad terms. Further complicating the situation is the stated purpose of kendo: "*To hold in esteem human courtesy and honour; to associate with others with sincerity; And, to forever pursue the cultivation of oneself.*" So, what should the problem statement be if the grading exam process is to be improved? As a starting point and perhaps a root problem analysis, we can try the following: "*The kendo promotion examination does not provide consistent results, nor does it provide the examinee with consistent feedback from the examiners.*"

Questions to be asked specifically by the examiners:

Are the results valid and reliable?
Validity is the degree to which an assessment measures what is intended. Reliability is the degree to which assessment results are consistent, particularly between different examination boards.

Are the examiners measured and given feedback?
Is there even a common understanding amongst any given board of what is being measured? i.e. *kata* vs. *keiko* vs. *written*. If federations can elucidate criteria, then the grading procedure can truly become an effective means for developing an individual's kendo. Examiners need to continually expand their knowledge in order to provide fair and logical results. Just as the *shinpan* judging a *shiai* need to make decisions that satisfy the spectators and competitors, the same is true of the *shinsa-in*.

An examiner should consider why each candidate fights two bouts at the *dan* level. If the candidate has a shoddy opponent for one of his/her bouts, this could skew the test result and cause both individuals to fail. By having a second match, either the results of the first match are confirmed, or there is a chance at redemption. *Shinsa-in* should understand this, and have the skill to differentiate between the two matches and judge the candidate's performance in its totality. If the candidate displays correct skills in one bout, but gives a poor performance in the other because the opponent is highly uncooperative (sloppy kendo), then that candidate should pass.

Exams are not just about successfully hitting people, but rather to show that you have mastered the criteria provided for a given rank. Even in Japan, some All-Japan champions have had a hard time passing their 7-dan grading. While *taikai* and *shinsa* should not be different, and the same criteria should be used to determine valid strikes, this may not be the case in reality. In theory, every candidate can pass, but in practice this does not happen. While at the lower ranks (2-dan and below) the pass rate can be 100%, at 3-dan it may drop to 50%, 4-dan 25% or less, and for 5-dan about 20%.

It is also beneficial to set minimum ages for the junior kendo population testing for the *kyū* grades. This allows for steady progress of juniors until they are old enough to attempt *shodan*, and appreciate the achievement should they pass. While progress might be rapid early on, it slows to a crawl over time. Gradings provide tangible goals for kenshi to strive for and achieve. Constant improvement—however slow—must be a prime goal for all kenshi. Federations would be wise to have promotion systems that allow for an appropriate pace for advancement.

The second part of this article in the next edition of *Kendo World* and will focus on "points for assessment".

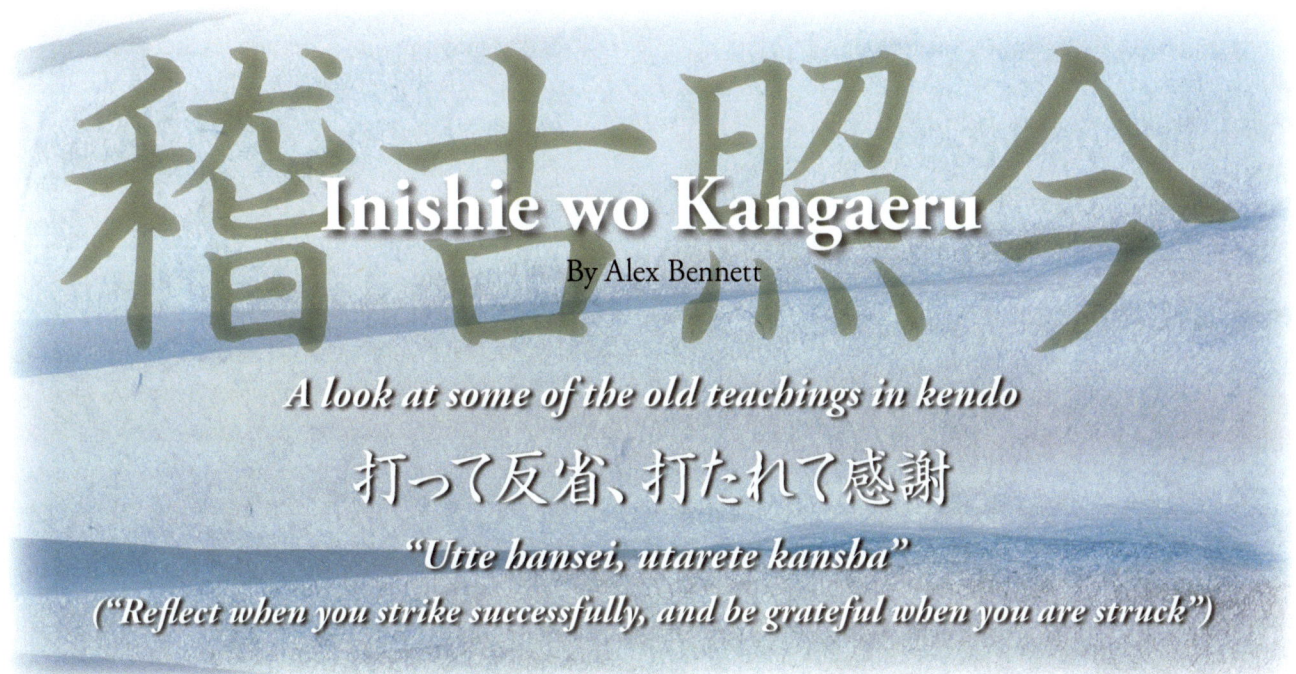

Inishie wo Kangaeru
By Alex Bennett

A look at some of the old teachings in kendo

打って反省、打たれて感謝
"Utte hansei, utarete kansha"
("Reflect when you strike successfully, and be grateful when you are struck")

If ever there was an oxymoron… If you successfully strike your opponent, is this not a time to rejoice and celebrate your success? If you are struck, the conventional reaction is surely to lament defeat, not be thankful that your opponent got the better of you! This old kendo teaching, however, holds the secret to improvement. When you score that decisive *men* strike in the final of the WKC, you have etched you name in kendo immortality. You are the world champion, and nobody can take that away from you.

I am reminded of the All-Japan Championships final in 2006. The two contenders were Uchimura and Harada, both policemen in the Keishicho. The two bowed to each other, and then faced off in *kamae* waiting for Shushin to proclaim the start of the match. "*Hajime!*" The bout progressed with plenty of exciting tit-for-tat attacks, but with no points scored by the end of the designated match time, it went to an *ippon-shōbu* sudden-death decider.

Then, Harada coaxed Uchimura into making a strike to *men*. Harada deftly nipped the *men*-strike in the bud, and whacked Uchimura's *kote* just as he lifted his hands. After making the strike, Harada kept his eyes on Uchimura as he moved out of the way with *shinai* at the ready for a possible counterattack. Meanwhile, Uchimura, acknowledging that his *kote* had been struck, and knowing that a counterattack was now futile, bowed his head to Harada as a sign of submission and respect. Shushin announced the successful *kote* point, and Harada was 2006's new champ. Both Harada and Uchimura returned to the face-off lines, not for a second lowering their gaze or losing eye contact as they crouched into *sonkyo*, sheathed their *shinai*, retreated to either side of the *shiai-jō*, bowed once more and then left the floor.

In ideal kendo form, it was impossible to tell which side had won because both had their emotions completely in check. There was no display of elation or disappointment. No smiles, no tears. Just the same deadpan poker face on both men. For Harada, this was undoubtedly the culmination of a childhood dream, and long years of gruelling practice. In any other sport, it would be completely ordinary, even expected for the winner to dance a little jig of joy. It would be just as pedestrian for the loser, Uchimura, to curse the heavens for his rotten luck, or fire poisonous barbs at the referees for their 'dubious call'.

Not in the case of kendo though. The loser shows no vexation whatsoever. To do so would be indefensibly disrespectful to the opponent and the spirit of kendo. Sacrilege. Uchimura simply acknowledged his

defeat, and bowed to the victor. He had been taught that there was a chink in his armour. Now, he had something to work on in his training. That was what the little bow after being struck meant. "Good shot my friend…"

Harada, likewise, did not boast of his victory. He may have won, but humbly acknowledged that it was by no means a perfect victory. As he vacated the court, I saw him turn his head in an embarrassed way toward Uchimura as if to say, "Sorry about that old chap. It was a bit of a crooked *kote* on my part, and probably didn't deserve to be the final point of the championships…"

A win is a win, and we certainly don't compete in kendo to lose! The kendoka, however, is expected to always seek improvement, and competitions are a vehicle for this. Winning is not the ultimate objective of kendo *per se*. Learning about your strengths and weaknesses is.

Both winners and losers showed no emotion as they exited the arena. A boring affair for professional photographers trying to capture those tell-tale expressions of jubilation and despair. But no, kendoka just thank each other again, and head back to the dojo to resume training (maybe stopping off for a quick beer on the way). This attitude is prescribed in the "Budo Charter" of the Japanese Budo Association. Article 3 states the correct attitude for competition. Competitors "must do their best at all times, winning with modesty, accepting defeat gracefully, and constantly exhibiting self-control."

Incidentally, Uchimura won the All-Japan Championships for the first time the following year, and twice since. He obviously learned from this experience, and "gratefully" took the lesson on board. Harada was surely pleased to add the All-Japan crown to his trophy shelf, but knew that he needed to do better than a slightly unbalanced *kote* strike against Uchimura's gallant *men* strike. He reflected on his win with humility, the way a true champion does. I know this for a fact because a couple of Keishicho sensei corroborated my interpretation of events ten years later in 2016.

TENDŌ-RYŪ

By Kimura Yasuko (17th Sōke of Tendō-ryū)

Introduction

Tendō-ryū is a composite school of *bujutsu* which incorporates an array of weapons, but it is the techniques of the *naginata* for which the tradition is most known for now. I received instruction from the 16th Sōke of the tradition, Mitamura Takeko, and was appointed as the 17th Sōke in 2013, three years after she passed away. Now in its 17th generation, the history of the Tendō-ryū extends back 450 years.

Early documents pertaining to the tradition are scant, and most of the ones in existence today were written in the Meiji period (1868–1912). Earlier scrolls mainly consist of *menkyo-kaiden* licences—essentially catalogues of techniques of which the finer details were taught directly from teacher to disciple. There are hundreds of techniques listed in the catalogues, but many have not been passed down and have been lost forever. Nevertheless, "*ichiomonji-no-midare*" has survived throughout

Tendō-ryū's history, and is the first technique that beginners learn.

Still, although it is the fundamental technique in Tendō-ryū, *ichimonji-no-midare* has no bounds in terms of depth. Based on the combat experience of the founder, Saitō Hankan Denkibō (1550–87), it represents the very essence of the school's teachings. Denkibō was born in Hitachi-no-Kuni Ide, present day Ibaraki prefecture, and studied the arts of the sword and spear under legendary warrior Tsukahara Bokuden. Denkibō's skill stood out among Bokuden's many students, but sensing inadequacies in his technique, Denkibō spent 100 days in ascetic training at the Tsurugaoka Hachimangū Shrine in Kamakura. On the 21st day of the 11th month in 1581, Denkibō dreamt that he was awarded a special scroll by the deity of the shrine, which contained the teaching for a divine sword technique. On the basis of this heavenly wisdom and the mysterious technique, he founded the Ten-ryū (Heavenly School), which was later changed in name to Tendō-ryū (School of the Heavenly Way).

Denkibō travelled the provinces engaging in duels to perfect his craft. His reputation preceded him and he became known as far away as the capital in Kyoto. It is said that he was even asked to demonstrate the secret technique *ittō-sanrei* to the shogun himself.

After his martial pilgrimage, he returned to his village of birth as a much more famous man than when he left. He was eventually killed by an arrow shot by Sakurai Ōsumi-no-Kami, a student of Makabe Dōmu of the Musō Shintō-ryū. The technique that he used to cut arrows that rained down on him before finally being struck was *ichimonji-no-midare*, and it was this that became the fundamental technique for his tradition. Denkibō's student, Komatsu Ichibokusai, who was with him to the end, eventually taught Denkibō's son, Hōgen, the technique. Hōgen became the second master of the school, and it was he who introduced *naginata-jutsu*, *nitō*, *kusari-gama*, *kodachi*, and so on into the tradition's repertoire.

Mitamura Takeko

Mitamura Chiyo

By the middle of the Edo period (1603–1868), the tradition had divided into several branches. Hinatsu Yoshitada learned two of the branches. He was invited by the lord of the Tamba Shinoyama domain to teach the tradition to his clansmen. His son, Hinatsu Shigetaka was more interested in the finer arts rather than military ones and went to Edo to study. Thus, the tradition was inherited by Shimokawara Yukinaga, and it was he who changed the name to Tendō-ryū. He moved to Tamba Kameyama to serve the Matsudaira clan, and from that time onwards the Shimokawara family became the sword instructors for the domain.

During the twilight years of the shogunate, Mitamura Akinori learned Tendō-ryū, and was to become the 14th master during the Meiji period. He was appointed to teach *naginata-jutsu* at the Dai-Nippon Butokukai, an organisation first established in Kyoto to preserve Japan's traditional martial arts. Akinori also taught at the Konishi brewery's dojo in Itami, where Tendō-ryū is still practised today.

Mitamura Chiyo became the 15th Sōke, and she also taught Tendō-ryū at the Butokukai school for budo instructors in Kyoto. In March 1941, the Butokukai announced its plans to create a standardised form of naginata to teach in schools, but Chiyo was vehemently opposed to the idea. She left her Butokukai post in protest and established her own school, Tendō Gijuku, to continue training future naginata teachers in Tendō-ryū until the end of the war. Her daughter Takeko became the 16th Sōke on her passing.

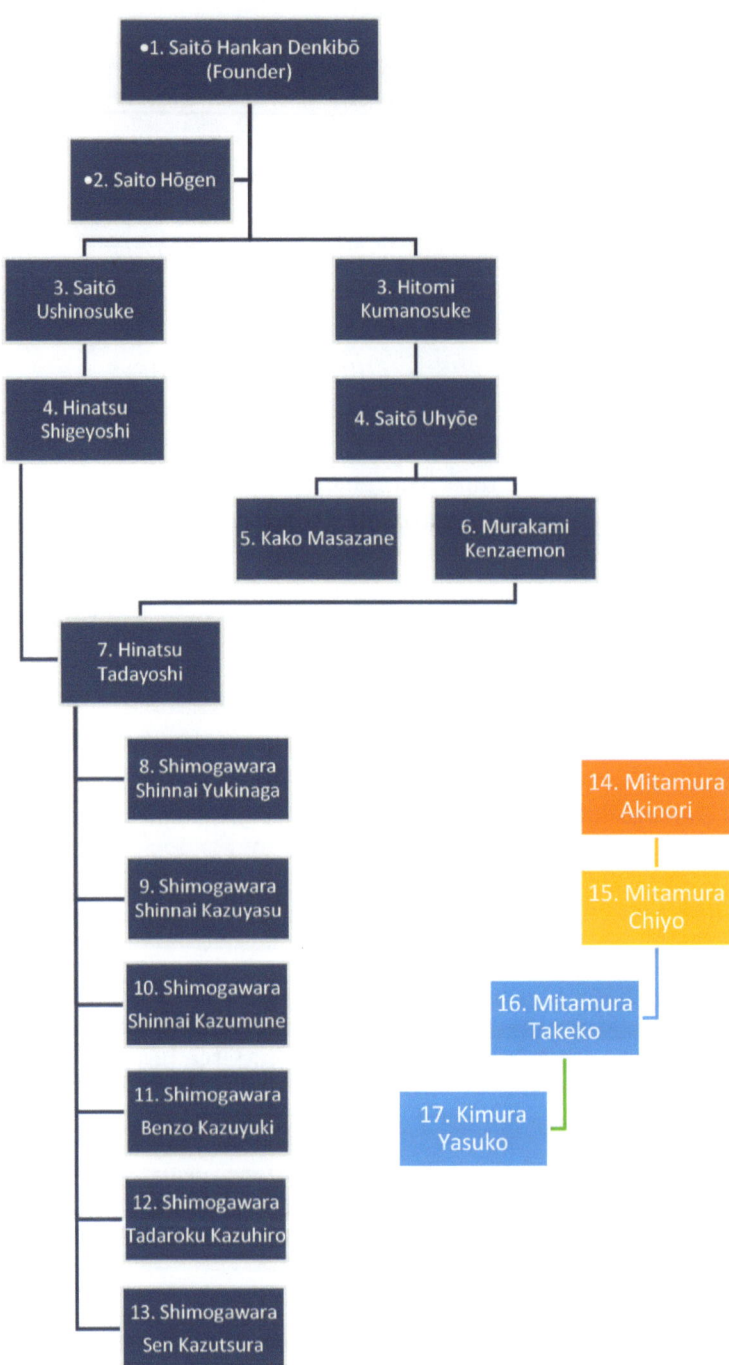

Outline of the Tendō-ryū Tradition

Currently, Tendō-ryū includes the techniques of *naginata-jutsu*, *kenjutsu*, *nitō*, *jōjutsu*, *kusarigama*, *kodachi*, and *tantōjutsu*, among others. Tendō-ryū was always headed by males until the 15th heir of the Sōkeship, Mitamura Chiyo. She was somewhat of a prodigy and taught at the Butokukai school and many other places, and contributed greatly to the dissemination of naginata throughout Japan in the pre-war era.

The Butokukai's teacher training school, Budo Vocational College, prepared students of the martial arts to teach at the nation's schools. Students in the naginata course would live together in a dormitory for one year, and studied Tendō-ryū intensively under Chiyo before they became school teachers themselves. This is when teaching methods for instructing large groups was developed, and was when counting was introduced into Tendō-ryū practice.

The *naginata* is a long weapon. It was originally written with the kanji meaning "long sword", but later became "mowing blade" because of the way it was wielded to mow down horses and warriors in battle. There were many different types of *naginata* depending on the era, and nomenclature depended on its length and shape. For example, *ō-naginata*, *shō-naginata*, *moroha-naginata*, *sendanmaki-naginata*, *nagamaki* (a cross between a *naginata* and a sword), and so forth. The *naginata* could be used to assail enemies from a distance, and was particularly useful for thrusting from far away. It became popular among warrior monks and women of warrior families.

Tendō-ryū Poems

The concepts and ideals of Tendō-ryū are contained in various poems which explain, somewhat cryptically, the characteristics of the techniques, and the kind of person apostles of the school should aspire to become.

- In tactics, the warrior needs to be flexible but strong, with eyes pierced and a biddable heart to seize victory.

- Secret of the art, there is nothing new; just have a heart of unceasing fortitude.

- If your mind remains forever ready to attack morning and night; the secrets of the school will flow through to the mind.

- Do not pass on teachings lightly to disciples; they must earn the knowledge.

- Do not fight over matters of good and evil; one of you will be wrong.

- The mind that listens for the frost on a cold evening will seize victory when confronted by the enemy.

- Tactics must be like rings; corners will be seized upon by the enemy.

- Martial artistry revolves around gaze, grip, and mind; never forget the gap between attack and defence.

- Never turn your back on the Way in anything; it is only then that one will become enlightened to the Heavenly Way.

Conclusion

Classical martial arts, or kobudo, form the roots of the nine modern budo disciplines. The rationale behind techniques has been protected and passed down over many generations. When practising Tendō-ryū, I often find myself amazed at how the techniques are so well designed. The 210cm *naginata* is not wielded with physical strength, but by correct body movement. When swung properly, the *naginata* is beautiful to behold and the techniques have a peculiar resonance. It is said that the footwork demonstrated by the 15th Sōke, Chiyo, was so sublime that the soles of her feet never became dirty. It was as if she glided across the floor. As the weapon itself is long, the movements are fast and crisp. However, this is reliant on where your centre of balance is positioned.

Kobudo does not typically have competition in the sporting sense as one of its objectives; the classical martial arts were essential training to prevail in duels and battle. The combat application and usefulness of kobudo disappeared after the Meiji Restoration (1868). Now, the classical traditions are recognised as Japan's cultural heritage with character development as one of its main goals. Through studying classical traditions, you learn to value the self and others, and get back to the roots of humanity. Self-development through the course of daily life and fostering an air of dignity is an important lesson that the study of traditional naginata imparts to us as we modernise. As Sōke of Tendō-ryū, I know that have a heavy burden of responsibility to pass on the wonderful wisdom that has been passed to me.

The Perennial Path to Perfection

by Alex Bennett

Although *Hagakure* (1716) is mainly concerned with the vicissitudes of mundane life for samurai in a time of peace, references that shed light on the winding path of budo are dotted throughout the text, and still apply to practitioners in the 21st century. It is easy to forget that the samurai were just human beings as well, and not the supermen that popular culture insists on glamorising them as. As humans, they had flaws, and when it came to the martial arts, there were those who showed awe-inspiring abilities, and others who were, well, just plain bad at it. Persevering over a lifetime of arduous training was, *Hagakure* advises us, the only way to transcend the constraints of mediocrity.

Vignette 45 in the first book of *Hagakure* relays the sage wisdom of one of Japan's greatest swordsmen, Yagyū Munenori (1571–1646). He was in his prime a century before *Hagakure* was written, but his teachings had a lasting effect on the development of budo theory. In fact, his discourses on *ki* and the mind are still profoundly influential in Japanese martial arts today. Under Munenori's tutelage were many illustrious apprentices, including the second and third Tokugawa shoguns, Hidetada (1579–1632) and Iemitsu (1604–1651), and many daimyo such as the Nabeshima lords of the Saga domain, from whence *Hagakure* came. He not only taught them the art of swordsmanship, but also how to apply the same principles to the art of governance.

"Training over a lifetime involves various phases. Unskilled men at the lowest level will make little progress at the start of their training, and their ineptness is obvious to themselves and others. Men at this level are of no use. Those at the middle level are still unusable, but are aware of their deficiencies, and are able to identify defects in others. Men at the upper level have useful skills, are proud of their degree of proficiency, enjoy the praise, and empathize with those who lack ability. This level has worth." (1-45)

Noteworthy here is the notion of showing empathy to those of inferior ability. How many senior martial artists, so-called sensei, can remember what it was like to be a wretched, discombobulated newbie? We have all been there, but success often stultifies our memory, and being bogged down in schooling beginners can be quite bothersome. An empathetic sensei is a true sensei, and one to whom humility becomes a trademark. Like the "boughs that bear most hang lowest," humility and empathy are prerequisites for the next level of mastery. *Hagakure* continues:

"Men who have traversed to an even higher stage of expertise in swordsmanship will pretend that they are unknowing, but those around them will sense that they have unmatched skill. This is probably the zenith of attainment for most men. Beyond this extends the ultimate realm that is impossible to describe in words. It becomes clear to the master that this realm is boundless, and his skill can never be perfect. With this realization, the master, being fully conscious of his imperfections, is neither conceited nor contemptuous, but continues travelling the path." (1-45)

It seems the better you get, the more cognizant of your imperfections you become. This is not taking humility to an even higher level. Rather, it is the unpretentious realisation that, as a human being, you are bound to be imperfect. Indeed, that is an inconvenient truth to someone of a swaggering disposition, and something not readily intuited let alone acknowledged. But, therein lies the difference between a skilled master, and an enlightened one.

As documented in *Hagakure*, Munenori sums it up nicely with his declaration that, "I do not know how to defeat others. All I know is the path to defeat myself. Today one must be better than yesterday, and tomorrow better than today. The pursuit of perfection is a lifelong quest that has no end." So, before plumbing the depths of despair apropos of the unattainability of perfection, keep in mind that it is not the end result that matters, but the

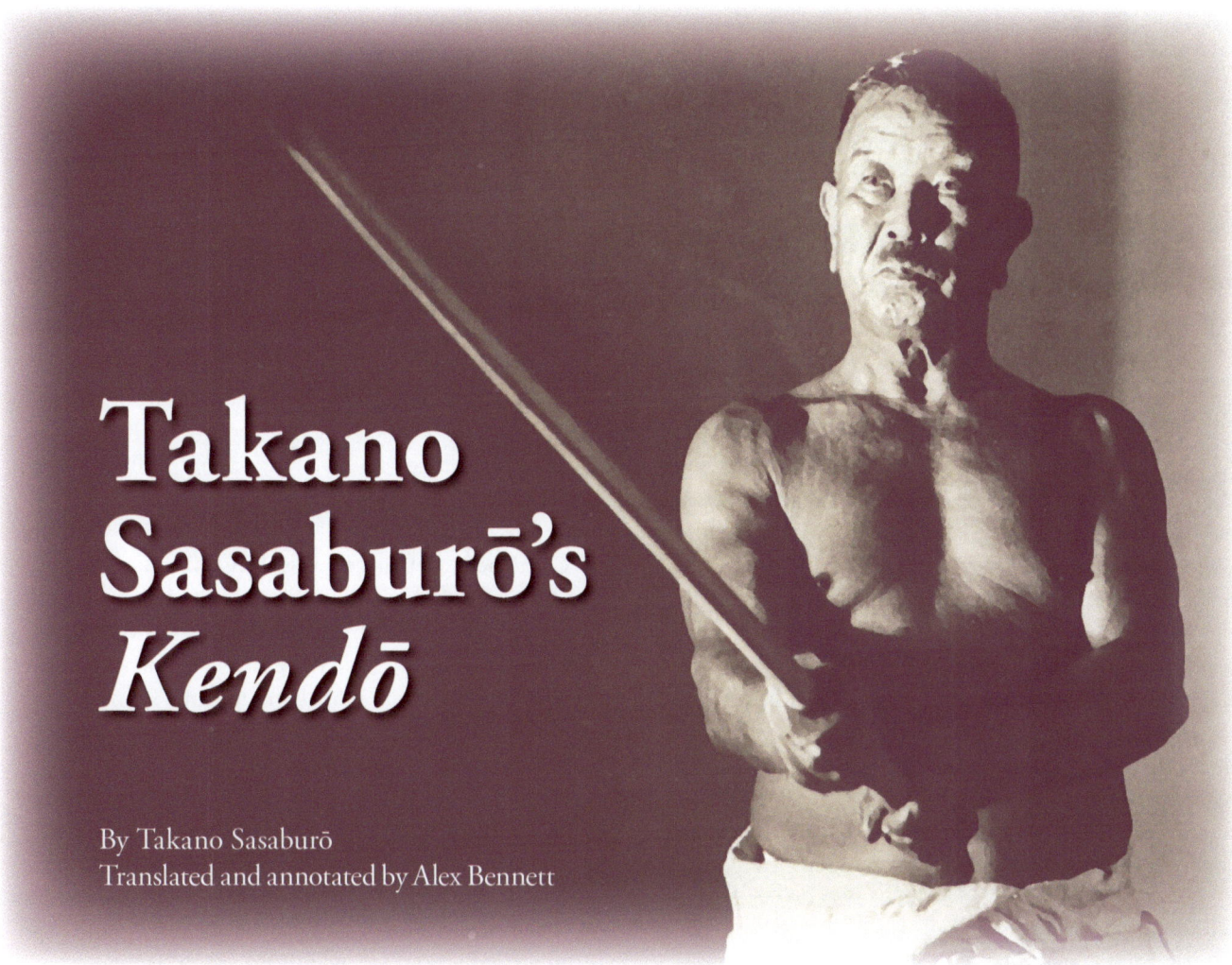

Takano Sasaburō's *Kendō*

By Takano Sasaburō
Translated and annotated by Alex Bennett

Takano Sasaburō (1862–1950) is considered one of the most influential pioneers of modern kendo. He was instrumental in developing the *dan* grading system for kendo, and was also a key member of the committee that created the Kendo Kata in 1912. His book, simply titled *Kendō*, was a *tour de force* in the creation of a uniform style for modern kendo, and is still considered a classic by kendoka today. In this series of articles, I will translate Takano's book, and annotate the text to contextualise its ground-breaking content. The following is the first two sections of Chapter 3 of *Kendō*. The remaining sections will be published in the next issue of KW.

Chapter 3: Training in the Fundamentals

Section 1: Basic Training

The objective of basic training (*kihon renshū*) is to impart the foundations of fundamental kendo movements to numerous students simultaneously, and ensure that they become proficient in order to progress. The traditional method of teaching kendo usually involved a master teaching his disciples one-on-one, and rarely were several students taught in a group at the same time. In the following pages, I will illustrate how to teach kendo to several dozen students in an efficient manner. Furthermore, not only was this system devised for instructing large groups, but much consideration was given to underlining the essential fundamental movements which will lead to an upright and unwavering posture, unrestricted movement of the hands and feet, and cultivate dexterity and stamina. The student will also learn how to strike and thrust, know the importance of correct interval (*maai*), identify striking opportunities, augment a strong spirit (*kiai*), and master kendo basics thoroughly and precisely.

When kendo is practised in large groups, there is always a danger that it will degenerate into a spiritless activity of just going through the motions. Therefore, the principles of kendo must constantly be reflected upon, and the exercises conducted with sincerity and a sense of urgency against the opponent. It must not be thought of as simply a physical exercise in which a sword is used in place of a dumbbell or Indian club.

If the initial instruction is substandard, students will quickly develop bad habits in posture and movement, which will be difficult to rectify later. As such, care should be given to proper instruction from the outset. To this end, the reasoning behind each movement is to be explained clearly—difficult techniques should be deconstructed and taught slowly at first, picking up the pace in accordance with the overall rate of improvement. When a satisfactory degree of proficiency has been met in the fundamentals, the instructor may then teach applied techniques, or a suitable combination of exercises. Start simple and work your way up to more complex movements, ensuring that students learn each step thoroughly. Once the fundamentals are mastered, students will then be able to train against each other and their fighting skills will improve in leaps and bounds thereafter. They will develop the ability to independently apply techniques of kendo to any situation they are faced with.

Section 2: Preparing for Basic Training
To commence with basic training, get the students to line up in formation keeping an even distance between each other. The instructor will position himself in the centre to demonstrate and explain the exercises, and students will follow the instructor's directives. Once they are able to execute the movements satisfactorily, divide the students into two lines facing each other at 9 paces apart, and instruct them in their roles. On the command, the students should be able to display ample fighting spirit as they advance to a suitable distance (*maai*) to perform the techniques in sequence. Warming up for basic training is conducted in line with standard callisthenics. The following is an outline of the procedure for running a kendo class.

(1) **Immovable Posture (*Fudō no shisei*)**	
Command: Attention (*Ki wo tsuke*).	The command must be given in a loud, clear voice. This is very important to convey the serious mindset of the instructor to students.
Outline: In conformance with Infantry Drill.	Both heels should be touching and in line. Both feet point out to an angle of 60 degrees, the knees are straight but not too rigid, the upper body is relaxed and leaning slightly forward with the shoulders pulled back naturally. The elbows should hang naturally with the hands touching the thighs, fingers lightly extended with the middle finger pointing down the side seam of the *hakama*. The neck should be upright with the head resting effortlessly atop, mouth closed, eyes open and looking to the front. In the case whereby a *katana* is being held, the left hand should lightly grip the base of the *tsuba* with the thumb extended over the *tsuba*, and the sword positioned naturally at the left waist.
(2) **Rest Position (*Kyūkei*)**	
Command: At ease (*Yasume*).	To change from "attention" to the "at ease" posture.
Outline: Step out slightly with the left foot and assume the "at ease" position.	After this, either foot can be moved off line, as long as the other remains in the original spot. The *katana*, should always be with the left hand, dangling down the side of the body.
(3) **Assemble (*Shūgō*)**	
Command: Fall in (*atsumare*).	Students are to be trained to assemble quickly and correctly. There should be no need to urge them to attention when assembling.
Outline: The instructor stands in the top position, raises the right hand, and calls for the students to assemble (*atsumare*).	Students will line up in double ranks. The instructor may command students to get into single or double horizontal rows or vertical columns as required. The head student is positioned directly in front of the instructor at a distance of six paces. All other students fall into line relative to the head student. (Explained in more detail later).
(4) **Numbering (*Bangō*)**	
Command: Number off (*bangō*).	Numbering starts from the rightmost student, and moves leftwards down the line. Usually the count will be 1, 2, 3. 4… Depending on the situation, however, the count may be restricted to "1, 2", or "1, 2, 3".
Outline: Numbering is usually conducted when standing in line.	The head student will turn his head to the left to face the student next to him. In the case where students are lined up in two rows, only the front row calls out their numbers. The back row pays attention to the corresponding number of the student in front.
(5) **Alignment (*Seiton*)**	
Command: a) Align yourselves to the right (left) (*migi* [*hidari*] *e narae*)… Stand at ease (*naore*).	Alignment is determined to the right (left), or toward the front.
Outline: In accordance with Infantry Drill.	Perfect positioning happens when students in each row are in line with the head student and standing up straight. When the head student turns his head to face the student on the right (or left), his right (left) eye should be looking directly at the student to his side, and his other eye observing the entire line. The interval between the students should be no more than the distance created when putting hands on hips with elbows splayed out to the side. The distance between the front and rear ranks is one step.
Command: b) Align to the front (*mae e narae*)… Stand at ease (*naore*).	Beginners are taught to gauge the appropriate distance by lifting both their arms up (or only the right hand if holding a *katana*), and lightly touching the back of the student in front of them. With the command to "stand at ease", students should immediately assume the "immovable posture".
Outline: The top student does not move. Other students stand one step directly behind the student in front of them.	

(6) Turn to the Right (Left) (*Migi [hidari]-muki*)	
Command: Turn to the right (left) (*migi [hidari] muke––migi [hidari]*).	Raise left toes and the right heel slightly, and rotate 90 degrees to the right (or left), and bring the right heel in line with the left. Be sure that the body (and sword) does not sway.
Outline: In accordance with Infantry Drill.	
(7) About Turn (*Ushiro-muki*)	
Command: About turn to the right (*maware-migi*)	Pull the right foot to the back with the right toes close to the left heel, go up on tiptoes keeping the back of the knees taut, about turn to the back, and then bring the right heel in line with the left heel. Keep the gaze steady as the body is rotated.
Outline: In accordance with Infantry Drill.	
(8) Advance (*Kōshin*)	
Command: Forward march (*mae e susume*).	When advancing, students must move with intent, and in a dignified manner. The length of each step should be 75cm from heel to heel (this can be reduced for middle school), and cadence should equate 114 beats per minute. In the case of middle school students, this will be 120-130 beats per minute.
Outline: In accordance with Infantry Drill.	Lift the left thigh up slightly, extend the arm, and with the toes pointing slightly outward, lean forward and step out 75cm from the right foot while gradually extending the arm. Do not bring the foot down loudly. Stretch the back of the knees and shift the body weight to the pivot foot and step through with the left. As the left foot touches the floor, the right foot is lifted, and as with the left foot, the right foot advances the same distance to move forward. The feet should not cross over, and the knees should not be lifted too high. Do not rotate the shoulders, keep the head and eyes fixed to the front and straight, and swing the arms naturally.
(9) Halt (*Teishi*)	
Command: Squad, halt. (*Zentai tomare*).	
Outline: Draw the back foot, back level with the front to stop.	
(10) Make Rank (*Kairetsu*)	
Command: a) Make rank with both (one) arms. *Ichiban [niban] kijun de ryōte [katate] sukima ni hirake*	
Outline: The head student does not move and the remainder lift both arms out to the sides.	Whereby the side-by-side interval between the elements is one arm's length, the arm closest to the head student is the one that is raised at shoulder height so that it just touches. As soon as they take position students then assume the "immovable posture".
Command: b) Odd numbers forward, even numbers back two paces. *Kisū mae, gūsū ushiro e ni-ho ni hirake*.	There are various ways in which the space between students one behind the other can be gauged, but the following is the simplest method.
Outline: This command is given in the case of single or double ranks (horizontal rows) when the distance between the front and back row is more than five paces.	Those who call out odd numbers will move forward 2 paces, and even numbers retreat 2 paces making 4 paces apart.
(11) Close Rank (*Heiretsu*)	
Command: Assemble in OOO order. (OOO *kijun––atsumare*)	When the directive "*atsumare*" is given, the other students quickly congregate around the head, fall in, and then assume the "immovable posture".
Outline: The instructor stands in front of the head student and gives the command while raising the right hand.	
(12) Fall Out (*Kaisan*)	
Command: Fall out. (*Wakare*)	
Outline: This is a sign of deference to the instructor, so after the command of "*wakare*" is made, students momentarily look at the instructor with respect, and after the instructor responds, students may fall out.	As falling out represents the conclusion of activities, it is important that it is conducted with solemnity.

Bujutsu Jargon

Part 10

Reference guide covering various bujutsu-related terminology

Bruce Flanagan MA
Lecturer—Kaichi International University

66 鯉口 Koiguchi

Literally 'carp mouth'; the name of the opening of a sword scabbard (*saya*) or blade sheath. Ideally a sword's collar (*habaki*) should fit snugly inside the *koiguchi* to prevent the blade from sliding out accidentally or from rattling around inside the scabbard opening. This offers a rudimentary safety measure akin to but not as reliable as the safety mechanism of a firearm. An action known as 'cutting the carp mouth / *koiguchi o kiru* (鯉口を切る)' is performed in preparation to draw a sword from the waist which generally involves breaking the seal by pushing on the handguard (*tsuba*) with the left thumb to clear the *habaki* from the *koiguchi* and allow an unimpeded draw.

67 正中線 seichūsen

The centre line of the body, sometimes called the *chūshinsen* (中心線), *chūsen* (中線), *nakazumi* (中墨), or often simply the 'centre / *chūshin* (中心)'. The anterior medial line, *zen-seichūsen* (前正中線), is the vertical anatomical line running externally down the front of the body which contains many vital points (*kyūsho*) susceptible to attack such as the eyes, nose, throat, heart, lungs, solar plexus, and groin. The posterior median line, *kō-seichūsen* (後正中線), is the vertical anatomical line running externally down the back of the body containing targets such as the cerebellum, spine, and kidneys.

68 新選組 Shinsen-gumi

Meaning 'newly selected group' (also 新撰組), the Shinsen-gumi was a security force comprised of unemployed samurai (*rōshi*) with exceptional fighting skills assembled under the command of the Tokugawa Shogunate in Kyoto in 1863. The role of the Shinsen-gumi was to track down and eliminate anti-Shogunate activities in Kyoto, the capital city and location of the residence of the Emperor at the time. Key figures included Serizawa Kamo, Kondō Isami, and Hijikata Toshizō. Forerunner groups were the Rōshi-gumi (浪士組) and Mibu-rōshi-gumi (壬生浪士組). The group's Edo (now modern day Tokyo) counterparts were the Shinchō-gumi (新徴組), or 'newly recruited group'.

 # 69 序破急 jo-ha-kyū

Originally a specialised term from Japanese performing arts referring to a gradual build up in tempo and speed or a progression in dramatic action or events. In oversimplified terms, the three phases are *jo* (slow pace), *ha* (medium pace), and *kyū* (fast pace). The concept is still used in arts such as *nō* muscial drama, *bunraku* puppet theatre, *gagaku* and *bugaku* imperial court music and dance, and *kabuki* dance drama. The principles of 'slow-faster-fast' or 'beginning-action-climax' can also be applied in a variety of martial art scenarios, in particular the sword-drawing motion of *iaijutsu* and iaido.

 # 70 霞 kasumi

The standard meaning of *kasumi* is the natural phenomenon 'mist' but it also refers to one's view of something being hazy or blurry. The term is utilized by many *koryū* arts to refer to specific techniques (*waza*) or stances (*kamae*) with long weapons such as the sword or staff. Stance names such as *kasumi-no-kamae* (霞の構え) are quite common, particularly in *koryū* arts featuring *kenjutsu*. Many variations exist between arts but some common characteristics of *kasumi* techniques and stances include: the weapon tip being aimed at the eyes of the opponent, the weapon being inverted or positioned in an unorthodox manner (often with the arms crossed at the wrists), or the weapon or arms being positioned to partially or fully hide one's weapon grip, weapon, face, or footwork. All of these subtleties aid to 'obscure' the opponent's view in order that they may misjudge timing or distancing.

 # 71 手刀打ち shutō-uchi

The proper name for the 'knife-hand strike' technique known commonly as the 'karate chop'. The first character is *te* (hand) and the second is *katana* (sword), and the two-character compound can also be read as *te-gatana*. *Sumō* wrestlers perform a special gesture called '*te-gatana o kiru* (手刀を切る)' when receiving monetary prizes in which they move their open hand through the air in a triple sequence of chopping motions as an expression of gratitude to the gods.

 # 72 武士 bushi

A generic word for a warrior or soldier who made their living from their fighting skills or military service. Often used interchangeably with the term *samurai* (侍) which refers to the warrior class that existed from the closing years of the Heian Period to the Edo Period. Another reading of 武士 is *mononofu*, which refers specifically to official soldiers who served the imperial court around the time of the Nara Period. Other generic terms for 'warrior' are *musha / musa* (武者) and *bujin* (武人).

Bibliography

- *Kendō Wa-Ei Jiten*, Zen Nihon Kendō Renmei (ed.), Satō Inshokan Inc., 2000.
- *Kōjien* (*Daigohan*), Iwanami Shoten, 2004.
- *Nihon Budō Jiten (Zusetsu)*, Sasama Y., Kashiwa-Shobō, 2003.

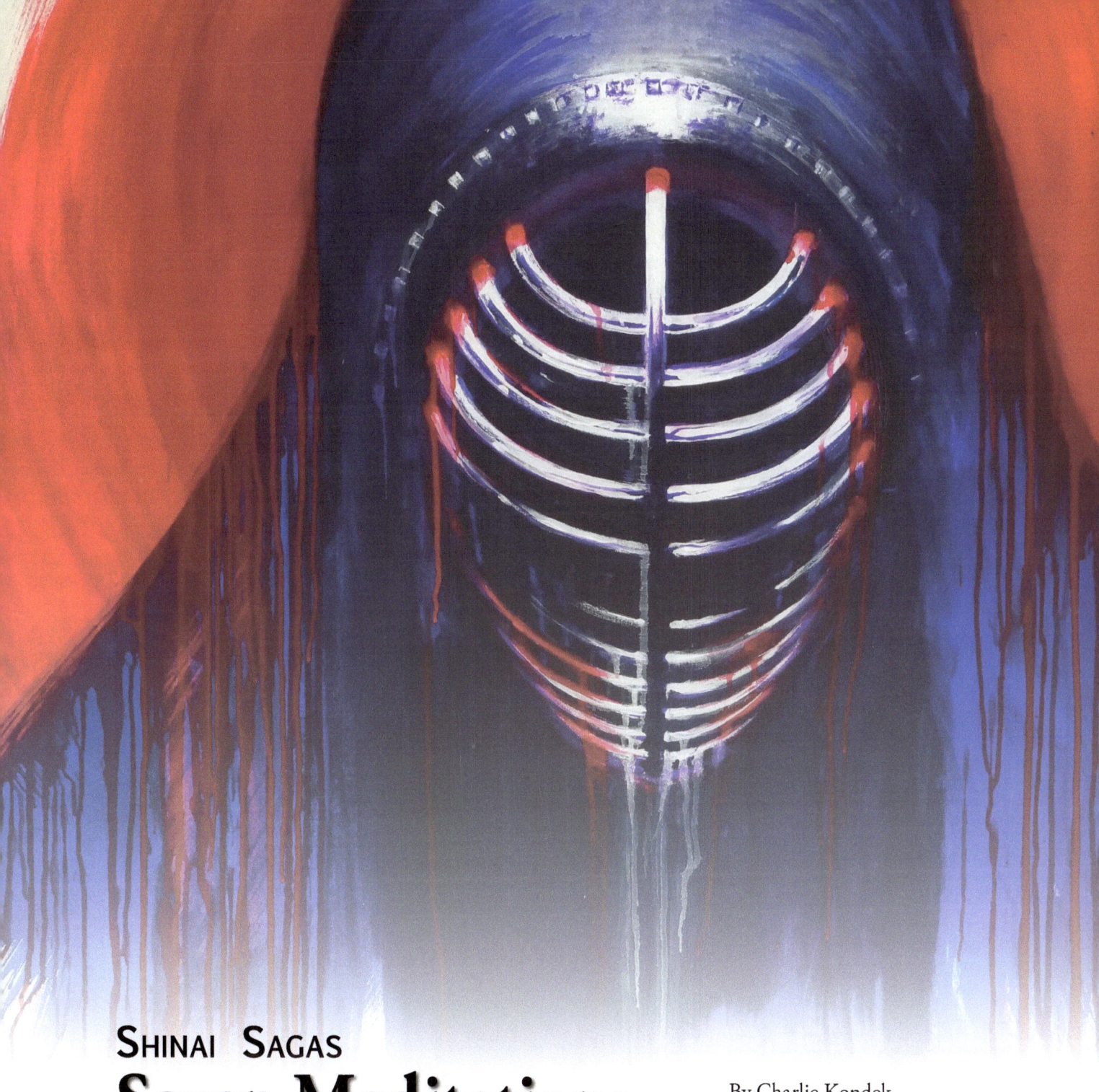

Shinai Sagas
Seven Meditations

By Charlie Kondek
Artwork by Phillip Solomon

A Cup of Tea

He didn't want to go home. Nobody wanted to go home, and yet everybody was weary. They were lingering, that evening, at the *izakaya*, several of the small tables pushed near each other and the chairs edged round the end of the table where the sensei sat telling stories and making remarks. They had practised, they had come to this place, they had drunk and eaten. The beer flowed, the conversation flowed, and now the electric shadows grew long in the corners of the place while Japanese television played on the sets in the walls, and the sensei, mixing *shōchū* and ice, spoke, half in Japanese, half in English. He had spent many evenings this way, at "second dojo". On one occasion, he had even seen one of the older Japanese guys nod off in his chair. Why didn't they go home? They didn't want

to go home. Something kept them here, some sense that the evening wasn't over. But now the boy that worked behind the counter was putting something into his hands. It was a cup of green tea, not too hot, in a Japanese style cup, no handles, a simple, traceable groove in the ceramic that he felt beneath his fingertips. He lifted it to his lips gratefully. It filled his chest with warmth and renewal as it passed through his mouth. "Oh, man. This is exactly what I wanted," he said. "How did you know?"

"It just seemed like you needed it," the boy replied.

Sink Like a Stone, Rise Like Smoke

He remembered a teaching about the purpose of *sonkyo*. Through the translator, the teacher had said that when you take *sonkyo*, you lower yourself to the earth, where all the *ki* is, in a field, and you gather the *ki* together into your lower abdomen. When you stand, it is rising up from this field. You bring the *ki* with you up from the ground. You remain connected to it, rooted to the ground, bound by your abdomen, as long as you remember to keep the *ki* there—in the lower part, not rising up into your chest. When you felt it rising, you needed to remember to push it back down. The teacher, through the translator, described *sonkyo* this way: "Sink, like a stone into the sea. And when you rise, rise…" The translator asked for clarification. "Like smoke."

This was an idea that occurred to him often when he fought. When he was hot and tired, and his arms were exhausted and he felt acutely the potential of his opponent to take *ippon* from him, he would concentrate his power into his legs, remember to push the *ki* down into the depths of his stomach, to his navel, and try to establish between himself and that golden field of fertile *ki* a connection that would flood power to his left leg. He would pull a deep breath from here. And hold back his *kiai*, maybe allow a short bark rather than a full throated yowl. When he felt himself slipping, he tried to reestablish his tether to the deep.

Time and Timing

Sitting in the airport, waiting for his flight, he supposed that somehow he had lost his ability to live in the rhythm of time. It wasn't that he couldn't manage time—he made his living managing time, his own and others'. It was that he couldn't manage his mental response to time, his estimation and appreciation of it. Much time seemed to have elapsed already. The decades that preceded the present moment seemed to have passed quickly. The time that stretched ahead of him seemed too little, threatened to leap forward abruptly, skipping entire years, ambushed by age. When he was trapped somewhere without freedom of movement, the time seemed to pass very slowly, until it was over, and then he wondered where it had gone. When he was free, he wished time would last forever, as if every day could be Saturday, and he made various spontaneous and involuntary efforts to stop time, caught himself standing or sitting and doing nothing but staring at something that interested him, usually the faces of his children, or a particular moment of stillness, like falling snow, the shape of a bell, or the late afternoon light through the branches of trees.

He supposed this was a symptom of middle age. He supposed that's why he drank, because time could be contained in the amber of alcohol, arrested for a while. The booze would slow him down enough to get back into alignment with the movement of time, the clockworks falling into place, moving forward with time instead of trailing behind it or, more often, racing ahead of it. It takes something like an airport to help us consider this, because airports, though beholden to schedules, exist outside of time. Probably because they disrupt our routines, and involve so much waiting, they enable us to keep still long enough to examine ourselves from the outside.

Too early for a drink, the sun muscular and hot in the windows over the airfield. Too much to do—later, later, when he landed, when he got where he was going, after his taxi rides, his meetings, a late run on the treadmill in the hotel fitness centre. But it occurred to him that he chased time, perhaps through professional instincts to get ahead of time.

He never stopped and stared time in the face, waited to see what time would do, and then reacted, pivoted to meet time, to take the right action at the right time. No, the urge to pounce was too great. He was always too occupied with imposing his own timing on everything. Maybe he could learn to experience it differently. More naturally. In time.

Death

Sometimes he examined death through the greasy window of exhaustion. It happened this way: he would be fighting in *ji-geiko*, *ippon shōbu*, and he would reach the limits of endurance. Pressing on, spent, breathing hard, limbs lamenting, blood and sinews in rebellion against his flesh, wanting only to give up after numerous exchanges of attack that did not result in a decisive win for either side, and unable to cope with the sustained terror of his opponent's next move, he would think to himself, "I would just like to be finished right now. I don't care if I lose the match as long as I can stop."

Immediately, at such moments, it would occur to him—all this, in the span of an instant—"Fool. If this were a real fight to the death, with real swords, you would not beg for relief from tiredness. You would claw and scrape for each chance. You would fight as if life depended on it." And he would find reserves of strength to continue the contest, to try to strike *ippon* on the opponent, defying limb, defying breath and an exploding heart.

This phenomenon gave him the idea that in kendo he could experience a symbolic death, a death without consequence, from which he was safe from any pain or finality. It occurred to him, dimly, that he entered into death without death's bargain—murder, without murder's black price—that kendo rendered unto him the power of the phoenix, to kill, to die, to rise again. It was the closest he had come, would come, to death, outside the occasional duties of a pallbearer. And he could experience it again and again. The result?

The result. Cognizance of fragility, finality. An appreciation of the differences between himself and the historical ancestors in the art. A fire. A knowledge that he could fuel the fire. A spirit of determination. A special kind of anxiety. Curiosity about mortality, a set of unanswered questions. A renewed sense of acknowledgment for the people in his life. For himself. An absurd sense of immortality. A view, anyway, of a foreign state.

Art

He wasn't sure when, but it occurred to him at some point that some kenshi practised kendo at the level of art. Looking back on this, trying to pinpoint when he had made the realisation, he determined it was a time when he considered the primacy of kendo among the pursuits of certain people he knew. By this he meant that everyone enjoyed activities beyond the necessities of work, civics, religious and family life. What these activities were further defined us as people. And, for some, kendo was one of a handful of hobbies, something done alongside, say, sailing or golf. But for others, kendo was the main activity. And not just a hobby, but something that was pursued to a more serious degree. That what was to himself a hobby, even a serious hobby, was, to others, art.

Or at any rate a higher calibre of artistry. For after all wasn't kendo by definition one of the Japanese "arts", the "ways"? So that anyone that participated was, to some degree, an "artist"? But here was how he identified the calibre of kendoist as artist—by degrees of seriousness. He compared it to other arts, say, painting. He himself could be considered a dedicated dabbler in water colour. Others were serious enough painters in oil to teach others or give exhibitions. Some, very few, were professionals, or academics at a level high enough where it could be said to be professional. Very few, indeed, made their living or most of their living from kendo.

So they could acknowledge all kendoka as artists, but divide them by degrees, by levels of dedication to the art. But that left an unanswered question. What is art? He brought the topic to several "second dojo" get-togethers, at one of which it produced a spirited row. First, they surfaced the dictionary definition of art (someone looked it up on their phone): art is something that is produced that is of no practical benefit. Some arguing ensued. Isn't a painting practical as a decoration, as a piece of furniture? A piece of music, isn't it practical as a pastime or an experience? Regardless, as a starting place, the definition would suffice. Sidebar: the "practical" aspects of kendo. Never mind. Then the real argument began. Nygaard wanted to blow up the definition. It wasn't fair that others could decide what constituted art and what didn't. But isn't this what we do in kendo, Mazurski wondered? Aren't there standards that others police? Damn the standards, argued Nygaard. If someone has the intention of creating art then whatever they create is art. Skenazy guardedly lined up behind this. Mazurski was opposed. "Then why bother having standards? Why bother having *shinpan*—that is the ultimate role of *shinpan*, art critic!" The group was challenged by the broadest considerations of what might be art: fine art, folk art, performance art, outsider art—martial art. In the end, there was no resolution, no acceptance of a definition of art. But there remained, for him, belief in degrees of devotion to the faceless god and accomplishments in his cult.

Action

After he scored *ippon* with *tsuki-men*, he could not really remember how he did it, though he remembered the feeling of it clearly. He could not remember why he chose this particular attack—he did remember having a difficult time breaking through the opponent's centre, and he remembered thinking, "I'm gonna jam this *shinai* into his throat." He committed to it totally, forgot in an instant all the inner warnings he normally gave himself when thrusting at the *tsuki-dare*—"feet and abdomen only, don't use your right hand!" *Tsuki-men* was his aim all along, but when the *tsuki* struck, he remembered thinking how solid and exact it was, how if he stopped there he might be awarded *ippon*. But already his hands followed the planted foot and the lancing blow that pushed his opponent back by bringing the sword tip up and atop the opponent's head, and with his wrists brought the weapon down swiftly and surely. His feet and a thunderous *kiai* followed. Red flags shot up.

Afterward he could not remember how he manufactured this manoeuvre, which was so unlike him, not one of the tactics he excelled in at all. He only remembered having the idea and then doing it. His opponent told him later that when he was struck with the *tsuki*, he couldn't control himself, his entire body was momentarily suspended, leaning backward, grass in the wind. When the *men* attack came he was helpless to block or dodge or counter attack. Both opponents, attacker and defender, marvelled at the synchronicity of it, the harmony in contrast to their usual flailings.

Signs and Gestures

The priest said, "In the name of the Father, and of the Son, and of the Holy Spirit," and the few congregants scattered among the pews made the Sign of the Cross and murmured echoingly in reply, "Amen." He liked to attend this early, mid-week mass at the towering old church in a disintegrating neighbourhood of the city. It was quieter. He could think more. And as he touched his fingers to his head, then his sternum, then to either shoulder, he remembered, as he often did, to invest the gesture with sincerity and meaning, to concentrate on what he was doing, saying. Because it was easy to make the motions and say the words without thought, at the prescribed time in the ritual. Because it was done so frequently, it was always vulnerable to becoming automatic and empty.

Musō Jikiden Eishin-ryū Riai

The Meaning of the Kata: Part 5

By Kim Taylor

Introduction

This is Part 5, the final instalment, of a series of articles about the meaning behind the *kata* of the Musō Jikiden Eishin-ryū (MJER) and the organisation of those *kata* into their levels and order. I claim no special knowledge of the thoughts of Ōe Masamichi as I was not alive when he reorganised the school into its present order. I simply offer my thoughts from a background of 30 years of practice in this school and in some other Japanese sword arts. Please understand while you are reading this that this is one person's way of organising and understanding the material. You are encouraged to read this, compare it with what you have been taught and what you understand, and come to your own conclusions.

The Third Level: Oku Iai

The first four articles in this series looked at Ōmori-ryū and Eishin-ryū, and the seated Oku Iai Iwaza. This article concludes the Oku Iai section with a look at the standing Oku Iai Tachiwaza *kata*.

Oku Iai is where the practitioner is introduced to multiple attackers and continuous attacks. These require a higher level of skill: a shorter and faster *nōtō* (the left hand is in contact with the sword's *mune* at the *monouchi*), sharper targeting, and more *enzan-no-metsuke*, which is needed to deal with multiple attackers.

If it is assumed these are the oldest *kata*, it makes some sense that both seated and standing *kata*, which are in fact similar to each other, are included. Many techniques in this set are actually quite simple but they are performed quickly and continuously with angled cuts and the consideration of environmental factors. They are simple but not easy to perform. There will not be a great deal of discussion on how these are performed, but rather the focus will be on what they mean to the overall instruction in the school.

Oku Iai Tachi Waza

The standing techniques will review and extend the lessons learned in the previous Iwaza set, as well as introducing some "practical" concepts. It seems that each level of practice includes a review of the previous set, thus giving a sense of continuity in the curriculum. The following two *kata* (Yuki Zure and Tsure Dachi) review some seated *kata* and "stand them up". This should be taken as permission to stand up any of the *kata*.

Nōtō

Yuki Zure

Tsure Dachi

1. Yuki Zure

This is a review, while standing, of the seated To Zume technique (see *KW 8.2*). Walking between two guards, we let them get a step ahead and then take the right guard followed by the left. All the comments on To Zume apply here.

2. Tsure Dachi

This is a similar situation to Yuki Zure, but the left rear guard is hanging back. As in To Waki (see *KW 8.2*), the opponent behind must be dealt with first using a thrust back as he is both close and watching our movements. Then we can return to cut the attacker at the front right, who was looking away as we dealt with the left opponent, but who is doubtless turning back to face us now.

When thrusting backwards, the heels are kicked out towards the rear so that the practitioner is even more quickly attacking the front opponent. This foot movement is equivalent to the movement of the eyes, which move

So Makuri

So Dome

towards the next target before the first is struck. For those who practise All Japan Kendo Federation (AJKF) *iai*, this moving on to the next target before the first is finished is a very different tactic. Beginners should not attempt this level of practice too early, especially if they are using *shinken*.

3. So Makuri

These are angled cuts performed while moving forward in a *kata* that can be performed in exactly the same way as So Giri in AJKF *iai*. Multiple cuts at different angles is a tactic used to overwhelm an opponent and therefore it should be understood well. The timing of one's footwork with a cut is critical and can be examined easily in this *kata*.

4. So Dome

This *kata* most likely originated with a past headmaster giving the class repetitive *nuki-tsuke* and *noto* exercises. This is simply *kihon-dosa* (basic practice) and students should not be afraid to do similar practice with other basics in the school. The need to control the hips is a great reason to pay attention to this *kata*.

An attack while the opponent is not ready is a useful tactic. Therefore, the well-educated swordsman is always in a state of *zanshin*, always ready for another attack, always ready to draw and cut once more, even while doing *nōtō*.

Shinobu

Yuki Chigai

5. Shinobu

This is a great example of *kata* that depends on the environment. We must have command of our body in any situation at all times, so a *kata* that takes place in the pitch dark is ideal. Close your eyes to do this one.

The concepts of distance, attack line, and timing of the cut are all well displayed in this *kata* as we move off the line, wait to hear the attacking cut and respond with our counterattack at the correct distance behind the *tachi-kaze* (the noise the sword makes as it cuts through the air).

6. Yuki Chigai

Again, this *kata* involves dealing with two opponents on the street that trap us between them. The opponent in front is too close too quickly for us to be able to respond well, so we strike first using the hilt, then draw and cut the one at the rear before turning back to finish the one in front. These 180 degree turns on the balls of the feet are very fast and require no leg movement. Without a proper understanding of balance and hip control, students tend to fall over when practising this *kata*.

Sode Suri Gaeshi

Mon Iri

7. Sode Suri Gaeshi

Since this *kata* teaches how to get through a crowd to attack someone, we should by this time be developing an opinion on how much iaido is "self-defence with a sword". This *kata* shows a way of getting past non-combatant onlookers without making them attackers. In this sense it is similar to Tora Bashiri.

The various ways to move between two people also teach how to deal with a living mass that must be displaced.

8. Mon Iri

This is another *kata* for dealing with opponents at the front and back, but with the space to begin by thrusting one-handed at the opponent in front, striking to the rear, and then the front again. Like in Tana Shita, there is an obstruction above (a gatepost) so the flat swing is needed once more. Since there are also narrow posts on each side, it is necessary to practise heel-toe turns when stepping through the gate repeatedly.

Kabe Zoe

Uke Nagashi

9. Kabe Zoe

In this technique, the opponent is struck down from a concealed position (around a corner), so it is vital that no part of our sword or body is seen before being ready to cut. This is the longest swing in the school, with an arc of almost 360 degrees. Despite that, or rather because of it, the cut is made while rising onto the toes to avoid striking the tip on the floor, so it is tough to develop power and maintain balance.

10. Uke Nagashi

Here we have come full circle back to a technique from Ōmori-ryū, but in this case it is used on a narrow path while walking. Forced to avoid an attack by cross stepping the left foot in front of the right, we are caught off-footed. It is actually easier to slide to the right with the right foot to avoid a strike, and this is done in the "extra *kata*" named Yurumi Uchi.

The type of Uke Nagashi guard used here is actually quite rare in this school, as body shifts or pre-emptive strikes are more common. Defending blade-on-blade is hard on metal swords, but the question is, are these types of defences more common in partner schools where *bokutō* are used? This can be considered in the partner sets.

Itomagoi 1

Itomagoi 2

Itomagoi 3

Oku Iai Variation

This level of practice has lots of variation from line to line, and dozens more within the lines themselves. This is a good thing, as students need to start breaking down the *kata* by this level to see how the *kihon* works best, so experimentation is encouraged.

Itomagoi

The Oku Iai finishes with three *kata* which are similar to Nuki Uchi or Makko but they are performed during a bow to one's opponent. This is revealing.

All three levels of practice end with this most pure expression of iaido, a draw and final cut in a single movement. This could very well have been the first *kata* ever invented.

While there are several other *kata* associated with the school (we practise six of them), this completes the core set of *kata* which exists today in the Musō Jikiden Eishin-ryū. I hope that the descriptions of the underlying theory of the individual *kata* and their relationship to the overall instruction methodology of the school that has been featured in *Kendo World 7.3–8.3* has been of some use.

THE YEAR THAT WAS 2016

By Seiya Takubo

March		
March 4–6	**International Budo Seminar** Nippon Budokan Kenshu Center International Budo University, Katsuura	

April			
April 1–3	**27th European Kendo Championships** Boris Trajkovski Sports Center, Skopje, Macedonia		
	Men's Individual	1st K. MAEMOTO 2nd A. PONS 3rd K. BOSAK / K. ITO	
	Men's Team	1st France 2nd Poland 3rd Sweden / Spain	
	Women's Individual	1st K. KOPPE 2nd S. Van Der WOUDE 3rd L. MEINBERG / A. MICHAUD	
	Women's Team	1st France 2nd Serbia 3rd Italy / Germany	

	April
April 17	**14th All Japan Kendo 8-Dan Holder's Invitational Championship** Nakamura Sports Center, Nagoya 1st Masahiro MIYAZAKI 2nd Masashi MATSUMOTO 3rd Isato MATSUDA Masahiro KOYAMA

K8-dan Miyazaki Masahiro-sensei scoring the winning ippon against K8-dan Matsumoto Masashi-sensei in the final of the 8-dan championships.

April 29	**64th All Japan Inter-Prefectural Kendo Championship (Team)** Edion Arena, Osaka 1st Saitama 2nd Ehime 3rd Osaka / Mie

May

| May 2–5 | **The 112ᵗʰ All Japan Kendo Enbu Taikai**
 Butokuden, Kyoto Budo Center |

8-dan division at the Kyoto Taikai

July

| July 2 | **50ᵗʰ All Japan Female Student Kendo Championship (Individual)**
 Nippon Budokan, Tokyo

 1ˢᵗ Momoka OGAWA
 2ⁿᵈ Ririko KINOMIYA
 3ʳᵈ Rikako IDE / Maki SUGIMURA |
| July 3 | **The 64th All Japan Student Kendo Championship (Individual)**
 Nippon Budokan, Tokyo

 1ˢᵗ Ryohei YAMADA
 2ⁿᵈ Yasunori KAIZUKA
 3ʳᵈ Daisuke H. MIKAMI / Rintaro MAKISHIMA |

<td colspan="3" align="center">**July**</td>		
July 8–10	**11th ASEAN Kendo Tournament** Suan Sunandha Rajabhat University, Bangkok, Thailand	
	Men's Individual	1st Oliver NG 2nd Masayuki SHII 3rd Erman ARDIANTO / Phanu PONGVANIT
	Men's Team	1st Vietnam (A) 2nd Thailand (B) 3rd Singapore(A) / Vietnam(B)
	Women's Individual	1st Pharwedow CHATAMRA 2nd Aimi MOHAMMAD SABRI 3rd Gin Jing CHING / Daphne Suyi WONG
	Women's Team	1st Singapore (A) 2nd Thailand (A) 3rd Vietnam (A) / Singapore (B)
July 16	**The 8th Women's Inter-Prefecture Kendo Taikai (Team)** Nippon Budokan, Tokyo 1st Osaka 2nd Gifu 3rd Okayama / Wakayama	
July 22–29	**43rd Foreign Kendo Leaders' Summer Seminar 2016 (Kitamoto Seminar)** Kitamoto City, Saitama	
July 24–29	**Gyokuryuki High School Kendo Tournament** Marine Messe, Fukuoka	
	Boys' Team	1st Kyushu Gakuin HS 2nd Shimabara Senior HS 3rd Fukuoka University Ohori HS Tokai University Senior HS
	Girls' Team	1st Nakamura Gakuen Joshi HS 2nd Chikushidai HS 3rd Fukuoka Daiichi HS / Shokei HS

July

July 30 — **5th Kendo World Tokyo Keiko-kai**
Meiji University, Tokyo

K8-dan Shigematsu Kimiaki-sensei (in *sonkyo*, left) instructing at the 5th Kendo World Tokyo Keiko-kai

August

August 2–5 — **63rd All Japan High School Kendo Championships (Inter High)**
Zip Arena, Okayama

Boys' Individual
- 1st Keita HOSHIKO
- 2nd Hyoga KAJITANI
- 3rd Tomoki KOSUMI / Hiroki TAKAYAMA

Boys' Team
- 1st Kyushu Gakuin HS
- 2nd Reitaku Mizunami HS
- 3rd Kokushikan HS
    Fukuoka Daigaku Fuzoku Oohori HS

Girls' Individual
- 1st Kana KOMATSU
- 2nd Maria ASANO
- 3rd Mizuho MATSUMOTO / Ami SHOUJIMA

Girls' Team
- 1st Nakamura Gakuen Joshi HS
- 2nd Sadaiji HS
- 3rd Kinkowan HS / Aso Chuo HS

September

September 6	**All Japan Police Championship 2016 (Individual)** Nippon Budokan, Tokyo	
	Men's Individual	1st Satoru OKIDO 2nd Satoshi NODA 3rd Kentaro OKAMITSU / Yasuki MAEDA
	Women's Individual	1st Mihiro ABE 2nd Mariko YAMAMOTO 3rd Kayo MORIYAMA / Masayo MIKI
September 11	**55th All Japan Women's Kendo Championship** White Ring, Nagano 1st Sayuri SHODAI 2nd Nanami ONISHI 3rd Mizuki MATSUMOTO / Mariko YAMAMOTO	
September 18	**62nd All Japan East-West Kendo Taikai (Team)** Koriyama-Sogo Taiikukan, Fukushima	
	Men's Team	East beat West 19–16
	Women's Team	West beat East 3–2
September 19	**59th All Japan Corporate Kendo Championship** Nippon Budokan, Tokyo 1st Panasonic (ES Kadoma) 2nd Fuji Xerox Tokyo (Main Branch) 3rd ALSOK (Tokyo) / Fuji Xerox (Main Branch)	
September 28	**H8-dan Masashi CHIBA-sensei passed away**	

Masashi CHIBA

	October	
October 8–10	**71st National Sports Festival Kendo Taikai 2016 in Iwate** Ninohe City Comprehensive Sports Center, Iwate	
	Men's Team	1st Iwate 2nd Tokyo 3rd Kumamoto
	Boys' Team	1st Nagasaki 2nd Kumamoto 3rd Iwate
	Women's Team	1st Iwate 2nd Chiba 3rd Kyoto
	Girls' Team	1st Iwate 2nd Kumamoto 3rd Ehime
October 9	**64th All Japan Student Kendo Championship (Men's Team)** Edion Arena, Osaka 1st Osaka Uni. of Health And Sport Sciences 2nd Chuo Uni. 3rd Uni. of Tsukuba. / International Budo Uni.	
October 18	**63rd All Japan Police Kendo Tournament 2016 (Team)** Nippon Budokan, Tokyo	
	1st Division	1st Osaka 2nd Kanagawa 3rd Tokyo
	2nd Division	1st Kyoto 2nd Fukuoka 3rd Wakayama
	3rd Division	1st Oita 2nd Ehime 3rd Aichi

	November
November 3	**64th All Japan Kendo Championship** Nippon Budokan, Tokyo 1st Yosuke KATSUMI 2nd Rentaro KUNITOMO 3rd Mitsuhiro JISHIRO / Keita MIYAMOTO

Katsumi Yosuke, the 64th All Japan Champion

November 13	**35th All Japan Female Student Kendo Championship Tournament (Team)** Kasugaishi Sōgō Taiikukan, Aichi 1st Meiji Uni. 2nd Nippon Sport Science Uni. 3rd Uni. of Tsukuba / Kokushikan Uni.

	December	
December 2–3	**The 5th Latin America Kendo Championship** Vina Del Mar Sport Center, Vina Del Mar, Chile	
	Senior Men	1st Jesus MAYA 2nd German DIAZ 3rd Sergio VELAZSQUEZ / Nelson UENO
	Adult Men	1st Vitor TACHIBANA 2nd Stefan DOMANCIC 3rd Marcos YAMAMOTO / Ronald OMASA
	Junior Men	1st Alex Daiki ITO 2nd Guilherme HAYASHI 3rd Eric KONISHI / Henrique HAYASHI
	Men's Team	1st Brazil 2nd Mexico 3rd Chile / Argentina
	Adult Women	1st Cristiane TOIDA 2nd Marina KODATO 3rd Barbara GARCIA / Caroline UEDA
	Junior Women	1st Danbi VELASQUEZ 2nd Yasmin YAMAMOTO 3rd Liara HIRAKAWA / Paloma ANZAI
	Women's Team	1st Brazil 2nd Chile 3rd Mexico / Argentina
December 4	**27th University Kendo Club Alumni Tournament** Tokyo Budokan, Tokyo Kendo World organised two teams of non-Japanese alumni to participate in this tournament.	
December 22	**Hanshi 8-dan Tadao TODA-sensei passed away**	

Other
In 2016, there was a total of 57 countries and regions affiliated with the International Kendo Federation. Four examinations were held for 8-dan with a total of 3,595 examinees. Only 30 were successful making a pass rate of 0.8%.

It is well known that Kendo is a popular activity among Police officers in Japan. In many prefectures there are specialist Kendo teams, known as the 'Tokuren', who are designated as the Police force's 'specialist' Kendoka. They can be said to be true Kendo professionals and these officers are among the best players in Japan and the winners of the All Japan and World Championships often belong to the Tokuren.

The Tozando Group have supplied many of Japan's Tokuren players with equipment over the years, which eventually lead to the joint development of our TOKUREN series of Bogu sets. The TOKUREN series Bogu sets have always been lightweight, stylish and easy to move around in, in order to maximize your Kendo performance. However, the latest Tokuren Z series takes it all one step further.

Unmatched mobility, made for competition

The new Tokuren Z series comes in two variations: the TOKUREN ZX GOLD and the TOKUREN Z SILVER, featuring 6mm Tight Cross-stitch or 4mm Tight-stitch stitching. This is a new type of stitching which improves durability and with the new type of padding we have developed, these Bogu form extremely well to your body. Only the slightest pressure will allow the futon to retain its shape, providing a great sense of fit. To make the Bogu even easier to wear and move in, our craftsmen have used all their knowledge and skills to make these the lightest Bogu so far, but without sacrificing durability and protection. We have made sure that strike zones are appropriately padded, to protect you against injury and unnecessary pain. We have also included in this Bogu the revolutionary 'IBB Safety Guard' attachment as standard that protects your throat against Tsuki, making it a Bogu that is thoroughly and truly made for high level competition. We have made the utmost effort in making a new practical, yet stunning Bogu series, so do check them out!

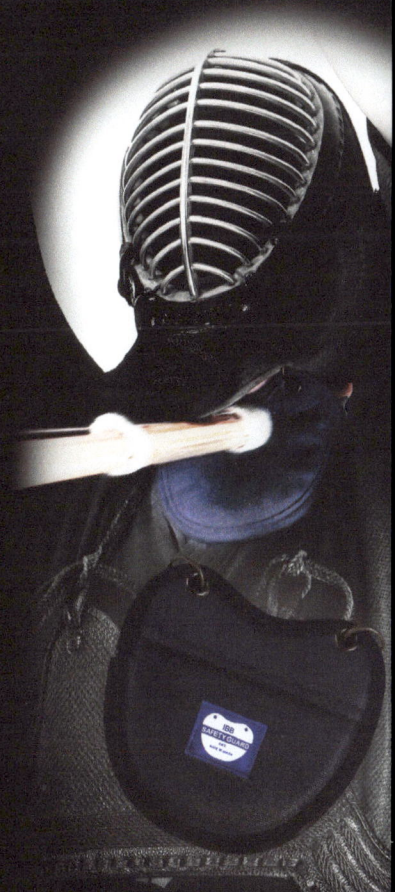

IBB SAFETY GUARD®

Our new patented 'IBB Safety Guard' is an attachable protector that protects your throat regardless of your head movements.
This will protect your throat from shock to the thyroid cartilage and injury to the carotid artery when receiving Tsuki. It also protects your throat against Shinai splinters should you receive a poorly executed hit or thrust. As you don't have to be afraid of the sword tip, you can charge in and aim for Men with high precision. Get it now, only from Tozando.

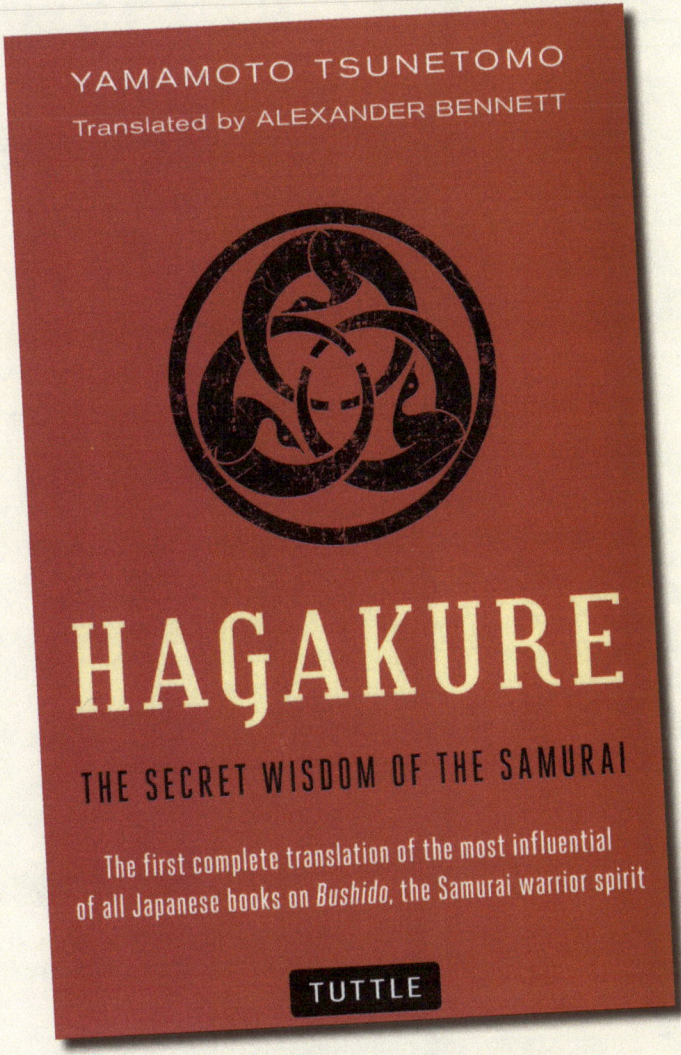

"Alex Bennett has produced the first truly authoritative translation and analysis of Hagakure—perhaps the most famous text ever written about samurai honor—to appear in any Western language. Simultaneously erudite and accessible, this volume belongs on the bookshelves of anyone—scholar or hobbyist alike—interested in samurai culture, or modern perceptions thereof."

— Dr. Karl F. Friday, author of *Samurai, Warfare and the State in Early Medieval Japan* and *Japan Emerging: Premodern History to 1850*

"[Alex Bennett] is the very best writer on martial arts alive today and [his] work needs to be showcased to the general public."

— Don Warrener, President, *Budo International*

"Dr. Bennett possesses a profound knowledge of, and deep insight into, the world of Japanese bushido. This expertise has been enhanced by his extensive practical experience of the traditional martial arts of Japan, and his proficiency in this domain is highly acclaimed."

— Tetsuo Yamaori, former Director of the International Research Center for Japanese Studies

"[A] strong point is a scholarly and succinct introduction that grounds the work in historical and social context, equipping the reader with a cultural map of Yamamoto's world. Footnotes provide valuable background and add resonance throughout, keeping names and familial relations straight, highlighting pertinent cross-references and generally rendering the work accessible to contemporary readers."

— *The Japan Times*

Search for "Bennett" and "Hagakure" on Amazon.com

www.ingramcontent.com/pod-product-compliance
Lightning Source LLC
Chambersburg PA
CBHW042017150426
43197CB00002B/53